CW00504636

A Book of Fruits and Flowers

*First published in 1653 and here reproduced in facsimile
with an introduction by C. Anne Wilson*

PROSPECT BOOKS · LONDON
1984

This facsimile edition published in 1984
by Prospect Books Ltd
45 Lamont Road, London SW10 0HU
by courtesy of the Brotherton Library
of the University of Leeds
who allowed their copy of the original
to be used for reproduction

© Introduction and Glossary C. Anne Wilson

Designed by David Grogan
Production coordinated by Carolyn Smith

Printed and Bound by Smith Settle,
Otley, West Yorkshire, England

ISBN 0 907325 19 X

Introduction

A Book of Fruits and Flowers, 1653, is one of the most attractive of early English household books, with its unusual illustrations, and its higgledy piggledy mixture of recipes for cookery, confectionery, preserves and medicines. But in spite of its air of old-fashioned quaintness, the book is surprisingly forward-looking in that its compiler had the idea of classifying his recipes under the headings of the particular flowers, fruits or vegetables which were prominent in them. Such an arrangement is not unfamiliar today, when the single-theme cookery book, which concentrates on either fruits or vegetables or fish or poultry, or some other well-defined group of foodstuffs, often has its recipes subdivided into sections which focus upon one individual main ingredient at a time. But in the seventeenth century cookery books were divided, if they were divided at all, according to the different processes of food preparation, or the manner in which the prepared dishes were served: boiled meats, roast meats, bakemeats, salads, banquetting-stuff (the last being the sugar-preserved fruits and sugary biscuits for the dessert course). The separate handbooks on preserving with sugar, and on the home distilling of medicinal waters, followed a similar pattern, with sections for the principal processes, such as the preparation of syrups, comfit-making, candying, and so forth; so the arrangement of *A Book of Fruits & Flowers* is decidedly unusual for its period.

The model for the layout of *A Book of Fruits & Flowers* was supplied, no doubt, by the herbals of the day; for these not only gave descriptions of plants, their habitats, and their medicinal virtues and uses, but in the case of foodplants they also often added a few words of advice on preparation and serving. There are many examples in Gerard's *Herball,* including the well-known description of the Virginia potato which is 'equal in goodness and wholesomeness to [the sweet potato], being roasted in the embers, or boiled and eaten with oil, vinegar and pepper, or dressed in any other way by the hand of some cunning in cookery'. *(Herball,* 1597, p 782). Thomas Jenner, who commissioned *A Book of Fruits & Flowers,* may himself have been the person who had the idea of combining the detailed cookery, preserving and medicinal recipes of the popular household book with the plant-by-plant approach of the herbal.

Jenner, who is named at the foot of the title-page, was a bookseller and also a print-dealer. From the mid-1620s onwards, he published a number of books on moral and spiritual themes, illustrated with copper engravings of appropriate emblems. He was a Puritan, and a supporter of Parliament during the Civil War, when he issued numerous broadsheets, books and pamphlets with a strong political bias. But at the same time he was a publisher of popular works, for which he commissioned, or pirated, both prints and texts. In the words of the prefatory note to the Rota reprint[1] of *A Book of Fruits & Flowers,* 'Maps and guides, newsbooks, drawing, writing and architectural manuals, almanacs, views, portraits, commercial stationery, all were grist to his mill as they were to his many rivals.' To these was added, in 1653, the present household book.

Although it contains virtually no description of the flowers or fruits, it is illustrated in the manner of a herbal or garden-book. And although the contents are of a mixed nature, the title-page suggests that the cookery and preserving recipes were the ones intended to catch the hoped-for reader's attention first; for details about preserving and candying the fruits and flowers, and a list of some of the culinary preparations to be found in the book appear prominently on the upper part of the page, while the ailments to be cured by the medicines are in smaller print (so as to fit them all in) on the lower part. The addition of medical recipes to cookery-books was common in the seventeenth century. At home, when the lady of the house (if she could write) transcribed recipes onto the blank pages of her own household notebook, the cookery recipes were often set down at the beginning and the medical ones at the end; while those for preserving were begun at a separate point part-way through. So the printed cookery-books tended to follow the same pattern, gathering recipes of all three types within

---

[1] The book was reprinted in 1978 at the University of Exeter for The Rota, an independent academic society devoted to the publication of Facsimiles of British Tracts of the Stuart era.

a single volume, and the more orderly ones confined those belonging to each genre to their own sections.

A Book of Fruits & Flowers was evidently a commercial success, and a second edition was published in 1656.

THE ILLUSTRATIONS

Seventeenth-century cookery-books were rarely illustrated, except by frontispieces. When illustrations do exist, as in Robert May's *The Accomplish't Cook,* or in the translated French book, *A Perfect School of Instruction for Officers of the Mouth,* they tend to be simple and rough. *A Book of Fruits & Flowers,* by contrast, has eleven fine copper-plate engravings, and is of special bibliographic interest in that it was printed in two stages. When the type was first set up, spaces were left at appropriate positions in the text for the engravings to be added later. Each engraving is surrounded by a rectangular frame. They all appear to have been printed individually and hastily, for several are crooked, and there are discrepancies in their alignment on the page between the prints in the Brotherton Library's copy and those of the British Library's copy from which the Rota reprint was made. In some cases (e.g. the aprecocks on p 35) the space left for the engraving was insufficient, so that the print had to incorporate the page number, which stands free above the frame of the picture in other cases.

The printer was Matthew Simmons, who had himself been a bookseller in his earlier days. He appears on the title-page only under his initials.

The problem of the sources of the prints is complicated and puzzling. The British Library catalogue says they are copied from Crispin de Passe's *Hortus Floridus,* published at Arnhem in 1614. The catalogue of the Library of Congress, however, draws attention to D. Franken's opinion that the illustrations of the second part of *Hortus Floridus,* which treats of fruits, are not the work of De Passe, but are by an unknown German engraver. The British Library also holds an incomplete and undated copy of *A Booke of Flowers, Fruicts, Beastes, Birds and Flies exactly drawne,* to which the date 1620? is assigned, and for which the plates were engraved by W. Simpson. It was published in London by George Humble, and the surviving part represents the second out of three books. The plates were republished in an edition 'with additions by John Bunstall' in 1661 by P. Stent. For both editions of this book, as for *A Book of Fruits & Flowers*, the British Library catalogue appends a note that the illustrations are copied from de Passe's *Hortus Floridus*.

I am most grateful to Marcus Bell, who kindly examined all three books at the British Library alongside *A Book of Fruits & Flowers*, and was thus able to report that only four of the illustrations of *A Book of Fruits & Flowers*, the olives, strawberries, aprecocks and cherries, are unequivocally derived from *Hortus Floridus*. All these are reversed, which means that the engraver copied what he saw in an existing print. In *Hortus Floridus*, plate 21, the 'cherries' of *A Book of Fruits & Flowers* are called 'damsons'. But Simpson had already used the true cherries of *Hortus Floridus*, plate 9, as his 'damson' in his engraving for *A Booke of Flowers, Fruicts ...*, and it is quite possible that one of his missing plates reproduced the damsons of *Hortus Floridus* labelled as 'cherries'. This could have been the direct source of the engraving in *A Book of Fruits & Flowers*.

Another missing plate from Simpson could have been the source of the lemon in *A Book of Fruits & Flowers*. The same lemon is used for plate 16 in the 1661 edition of *A Booke of Flowers, Fruicts ...*, and it may well have been present among Simpson's engravings for the earlier edition. The rose used for *A Book of Fruits & Flowers* is certainly one of Simpson's engravings, and it reappears in the 1661 edition. Marcus Bell noticed that in the plates of *A Booke of Flowers, Fruicts ...* various insects have been added to both the lemon and the rose (which do not, of course, appear in our picture in *A Book of Fruits & Flowers*); and that animals and, especially in the 1661 edition, a great many birds have also been added in a number of cases to the illustrations which are common to both editions and to *Hortus Floridus*. So it looks as though the original plates for that book may have survived for a considerable time, and have been reworked with additional fauna for each edition of *A Booke of Flowers, Fruicts ... [etc]*.

Of the remaining five pictures in *A Book of Fruits & Flowers*, the quince may be a debased form of the *Hortus Floridus* version, though the leaves are quite different. The picture evidently failed to give satisfaction because too much space had been left within the upper part of the frame. The engraver therefore added various examples of the letter Q (including also Hebrew cof) to occupy the vacant space, and thereafter was careful to make his engravings fit more exactly into the area enclosed by the frame. The medlars may be a distant, freehand copy of those in *Hortus Floridus*, though the positioning of the fruits is different. Perhaps both they and the quinces were copied from lost prints that were themselves at one remove at least from *Hortus Floridus*. The violets and the cowslips are from a totally different, unidentified source, and the cowslips are anatomically incorrect, compared with those of *Hortus Floridus* in which the head is formed from a single group of flowers, and none grow from the main stalk.

Lastly, the beans are not what they seem. They are not copied from *Hortus Floridus* where the bean picture, later reused in *A Booke of Flowers, Fruicts* ... displays Old World beans, with the pods growing upwards and the label *Faba sativa* as further confirmation. The bean-pods of *A Book of Fruits & Flowers* also grow upwards, but they are joined to the main stem, flower, and flower-bud, in an odd fashion, and appear to have two little roots protruding from the point of junction. If the picture is turned upside-down, however, it will be seen that these bean-pods are hanging downwards from their stalk in the manner of runner-beans. The two roots then become broken ends of a main stalk, from which other beans formerly grew below and above the ones in the picture. New World *Phaseolus* beans of similar type are shown in Gerard's *Herball*, 1597 (p 1038), where there is also an illustration of the fruit of the Brasile Kidney Beane in the form of two ripe pods, one partly open (p 1040). In Gerard's picture they are pointing upwards, in the opposite direction to that in which they would have grown, just like the bean-pods in *A Book of Fruits & Flowers*. Gerard's engraving may have influenced the source from which the 'beanes' in *A Book of Fruits & Flowers* were copied. Alternatively, two real *Phaseolus* bean-pods may have been portrayed from life. But however the bean was shown in the source, *Phaseolus* beans were still too rare in England for the engraver of the plate for *A Book of Fruits & Flowers* to recognise them for what they were, and he therefore reproduced and labelled his two bean-pods upside down, growing in the manner of the *Faba* beans he already knew.

One other curiosity may be noted. The olives are used to illustrate the recipes for almonds. No picture of almonds appears in the book, and there are no recipes incorporating olives.

THE CONTENT

The position of the prints in the book was, of course, dictated by the layout of the text, which was so arranged that a space was left for each print to appear on the upper part of a page close to the recipes belonging to its fruit or flower. But although the compiler of *A Book of Fruits & Flowers* follows his classificatory method through the earlier part of the book, with lemons, quinces, roses, barberries, almonds, strawberries and artichokes all displaying their versatility in the made dishes of cookery, in preserves and syrups and in medicines, his system then breaks down as he inserts nearly three pages (pp 16–19) of miscellaneous medical recipes under the heading OF MEDICINES in large capitals. Several of these remedies include herbs, but there is no attempt to group them according to a key herbal ingredient. Thereafter other batches of unrelated medical recipes are inserted after the entries for violets, cowslips and beans. Then come apricots, preserved in different ways. But under the next heading, 'Of lillies', only the way to use oil of lilies is given, followed by three general recipes for candying all kinds of flowers, stalks and roots. 'Of grapes' heads a single recipe for a syrup based on the Italian *agresto,* or verjuice of unripe grapes.

It is followed by a large new heading, in capitals: OF PURGES. But only the first item in this section is a purge, and it is described as, 'A purge to drive out the French Pox, before you use the ointment'. The French pox was, of course, syphilis, which had reached Europe from the Americas, and, like French beans, had reputedly arrived in France before it made its way into England. The next two paragraphs concern the ointment, based on litharge (yellow oxide of lead), and its application; and the last recipe in the section is a cure for a totally different ailment: a remedy 'for a paine in the ears'.

One or two unrelated recipes had already been inserted in the earlier part of the book; under cherries, for instance, there are instructions both for a fine pippin tart, and for a tart of butter and eggs coloured green with spinach juice. But in the final pages, a new large heading OF COOKERY introduces a short section (pp 46–49) of general cookery recipes. Among them are also two recipes for producing cast-sugar objects in moulds, and the barley cream recipe from p 11 making its second appearance; and the whole section brings the book to a close.

The old-fashioned air of some of the cookery and medical recipes is genuine enough. At least thirteen of them had been printed more than fifty years earlier in Thomas Dawson's *The Good Huswives Iewell, newly augmented,* 1596. This book contains both culinary recipes and medical remedies, and examples of both can be found scattered through *A Book of Fruits & Flowers:-* To boyle a capon with oranges and lemmons (p 3); A lemmond sallet (p 3); A maid dish of hartechoakes (p 17); A good plaister for the strangury (p 22); To defend humours (p 28); A powder for wounds (p 32); To make a water for all wounds and cankers (p 34); To make all manner of fruit tarts (p 40); A close tart of cherries (p 41); A tart of medlers (p 45); A sallet of all kinds of hearbs (p 49); and, To make fritter-stuffe (p 49).

There are many minor discrepancies between the Dawson recipes and the versions of them given in *A Book of Fruits & Flowers.* It may be that the intermediary was a manuscript recipe-book into which someone had copied favourite recipes. But it is equally possible that a badly-printed pirated collection of Dawson recipes was in circulation, and was the source of the material in *A Book of Fruits & Flowers.* Whatever the cause, these recipes are not exact copies of their originals, and in one or two cases the sense has suffered. More than one mistake has crept into 'To boyle a capon ...' (p 3). Dawson's recipe runs: '... and put them into your best broth of mutton or capon with prunes or currants and three or four dates, and when they have been well sodden put whole pepper, great mace, a good piece of sugar ...'. The version of *A Book of Fruits & Flowers* is: '... and put them into your best broth of mutton or capon with prunes or currants three or four *dayes,* and when they have been well sodden, *cut* whole pepper, great mace and a *great* piece of sugar ...'.

Dawson's 'Powder peerless for wounds' ('A powder for wounds' in *A Book of Fruits & Flowers)* had been copied by him from a still earlier manuscript source, and it ends: '... and lay scrapte Linte about it and a plaister of Duiflosius next underneath written, and it &c. The rest wanteth.' This was altered in *A Book of Fruits & Flowers* (p 32) to ' ... and lay scrap't lint about it, and a Plainer of Disklosions next upon it, and it will heale it'. Medical recipes, with their Latinized Greek terms, suffered even more from miscopying than culinary ones. Numerous recopyings compounded the problem, for some of the recipes had their origins very far back. Nevertheless, they continued to be repeated as space-fillers in the printed collections long after they had become too garbled to have any practical value. [For the plaster itself, see Glossary under PLAINER ...]

A further scattering of recipes owes its origin to the anonymous *A Closet for Ladies and Gentlewomen*, first published in 1608, though several other editions were issued between then and 1656. Most of these recipes had been altered considerably between the time when they were first printed in *A Closet ...* and the time when they reappeared in print in *A Book of Fruits & Flowers*. Nevertheless each retains the basic structure and enough of the original phraseology to make it plain that their source, perhaps at some removes, has been *A Closet ...* . The recipes are:- To preserve Orenges and Lemmons *(A Book of Fruits & Flowers*, p 2); To make printed quidony of quinces (p 6); To make paste of violets or any kind of flowers (p 21) – this recipe is rather different from the one in *A Closet ...* , yet all the same ingredients are present in both, as are the alabaster mortar, the printing in moulds, and the gilding of the paste flowers, which suggests a rewriting of the earlier recipe in the light of practical experience; To make the rock candies upon all spices, flowers, and roots (p 37), which expands the recipe, 'To candy all manner of flowers, fruits and spices, the clear rock-candy' in *A Closet...*, again in a fashion which indicates that practice of the recipe had produced modifications; To make snow (p 46); and, finally, To make all kinds of turned works in fruitage, hollow (p 48), where three-piece moulds of stone or pewter ware are substituted for the three- piece moulds of alabaster in *A Closet ...*, while the method whereby the filled and closed moulds are turned about in the hand in *A Closet ...* is changed (probably as the result of miscopying at some point) so that they are turned 'round about your head' in *A Book of Fruits & Flowers*.

But the source of the majority of the recipes in *A Book of Fruits and Flowers* was still a puzzle until I made a chance discovery while I was consulting, for another purpose, *The Ladies Cabinet Enlarged and Opened* by the late Lord Ruthven, 1654. Several of the recipes in that book seemed familiar; and, sure enough, they all proved to be present in *A Book of Fruits & Flowers*. The next question was: did they form the material of the enlargement of *The Ladies Cabinet*,

THE
LADIES CABINET
ENLARGED and
OPENED:

Containing
Many Rare Secrets and Rich Orna-
ments of several kindes, and
different uses.

Comprized
Under three general Heads.

Viz.
of
{
1. Preserving, Conserving, Candying, &c
2. Physick and Chirurgery.
3. Cookery and Houswifery.

Whereunto is added,
Sundry Experiments, and choice Ex-
tractions of Waters, Oyls, &c.

Collected and practised;
By
the late Right Honorable and
Learned Chymist,

The Lord RUTHUEN.

With
A particular Table to each Part.

London, Printed by T.M. for *M.M. G. Bedell*,
and *T. Collins*, at the middle Temple;
Gate, Fleet-street. 1654.

*The title page of the Brotherton Library copy of
the 1654 edition of Lord Ruthven's book, which
provided the clue to the provenance of many of
the recipes in* A Book of Fruits and Flowers

and had the enlarger purloined them from *A Book of Fruits &
Flowers;* or was the purloining done by Thomas Jenner from the
original edition of Ruthven's book, titled, simply, *The Ladies
Cabinet Opened,* and published in 1639?

Marcus Bell kindly checked for me a long list of examples of
recipes common to the two later books with the text of the very
rare 1639 *The Ladies Cabinet Opened* in the British Library (this
book is not held in the Brotherton Library). He reported that every

one was present in that first edition of *The Ladies Cabinet*, identical both in title and in the wording of the recipe-text. There was no need to look any further for the principal source of the recipes in *A Book of Fruits & Flowers*.

All the medical recipes there come from *The Ladies Cabinet Opened*, except for the small number already recorded as derived from Dawson's *The Good Huswives Iewell*. All the cookery recipes in the final section of *A Book of Fruits & Flowers* are also from *The Ladies Cabinet Opened*, except for the last two, which come from Dawson's book. Nearly all the remaining recipes are from *The Ladies Cabinet Opened*, apart from the few for salads, tarts and made dishes noted in the list of items taken from Dawson. The altered recipes from *A Closet for Ladies and Gentlewomen* were already in *The Ladies Cabinet Opened* in a format identical to that in *A Book of Fruits & Flowers*. The alterations had therefore been made earlier, before the recipes were incorporated in the book of 1639.

A few inconsistencies remain, which indicate the speed and carelessness with which the recipes in *The Ladies Cabinet Opened* were marked up for the printer. 'The use of the oyle of wormwood, and oyle of mint' has been put into the section 'Of cowslips' *(A Book of Fruits & Flowers, p 25)* because the instructions followed after those for 'Oyle of cowslips' in *The Ladies Cabinet Opened*. But 'Sweet bagges to lay amongst linnen', which follows 'To make past of lemmons' (p 2) is separated from that recipe by three pages and twelve intervening items in *The Ladies Cabinet Opened*. The only likely explanation is that the compiler, whether Thomas Jenner himself, or Matthew Simmons following Jenner's instructions, read and marked the headings of the recipes in *The Ladies Cabinet Opened* so quickly that he noticed only the keywords, and even so misread 'linnen' for 'Lemon'.

To trace the sources of all the recipes in *The Ladies Cabinet Opened* would require much further research, for Lord Ruthven cast his net widely, and probably included material supplied by friends from household books which had not been in print before. He also consulted many published books. The statement on the use of conserve of marigolds on p 39 of *A Book of Fruits & Flowers*, which was in *The Ladies Cabinet Opened*, had come originally from Gerard's *Herball*; but Lord Ruthven had culled other 'uses' – of the oil of lilies (on p 36), of the oil of violets, and of the conserve of violets and cowslips (on p 20) from elsewhere. His version of 'To make fine white leach of almonds' *(A Book of Fruits & Flowers,* p 12) goes back ultimately to Sir Hugh Plat's *Delightes for Ladies,* 1602, and many later editions, though it had already been expanded by the time it was added to *The Ladies cabinet* in 1639. Lord Ruthven does not, however, appear to have included in his collection those recipes from Thomas Dawson's book of 1596 which are repeated in *A Book of Fruits and Flowers*

A BOOK OF FRUITS & FLOWERS

The picture that emerges of the birth of *A Book of Fruits & Flowers* is of Thomas Jenner in possession of a miscellaneous group of about a dozen prints of fruits and flowers, including four illustrations from de Passe's *Hortus Floridus* and others from Simpson's *A Booke of Flowers, Fruicts* ... and from elsewhere, and also of a copy of Ruthven's *The Ladies Cabinet Opened* of 1639, plus either a manuscript copy or a small, badly-printed collection of recipes pirated from Dawson's *The Good Huswives Iewell* of 1596. He conceives the idea of rearranging the recipes in *The Ladies Cabinet Opened* to match his pictures, and he engages an engraver to copy the prints. Due to a misunderstanding, the engraver copies the olives instead of, or in the absence of, the almonds; or perhaps twelve prints were commissioned, and when no matching recipes were found for the olives, it was decided they should be omitted, but through mischance the almonds were discarded instead.

Jenner decides to add a few recipes from his version of *The Good Huswives Iewell* to his text for good measure, but then he realizes that he cannot, even so, find enough medical recipes to correspond to his chosen fruits and flowers, or even to those additional ones which he proposes to include without any illustrations. He therefore instructs the printer to feed in large groups of unrelated medical recipes from *The Ladies Cabinet Opened* through the middle pages of the text, interspersing them with the fruit and flower recipes. When enough have been fed in to bulk the volume sufficiently, he stops them. But he feels the book is still rather unbalanced as a household manual, for several aspects of cookery have not been represented. So as a tailpiece he puts in a further selection of Lord Ruthven's cookery recipes, plus two more from Thomas Dawson's book; and then he feels he can set down, in large capitals, the word FINIS. Thus, or in some very similar manner, Thomas Jenner pirated and organized his material for *A Book of Fruits & Flowers*.

★ ★ ★ ★ ★ ★ ★

THE ORIGINAL COPY

The copy of *A Book of Fruits & Flowers* from which our facsimile edition was made belongs to the John F. Preston collection of early English cookery books in the Brotherton Library at the University of Leeds. The collection was given to the Library in 1961, and it is housed alongside the Brotherton Library's other collection of historic cookery books, the Blanche Leigh collection, comprising European as well as English books, which was presented to the Library in the 1930s. Books from both collections may be consulted in the Library by outside readers.

Mr Preston now lives in Sussex. He was delighted to hear that a new facsimile was to be made, so that *A Book of Fruits & Flowers*, with its attractive pictures and unusual recipes, would once more be available to cooks and conserve-makers and those who take pleasure in learning about the domestic life of our forebears.

C. ANNE WILSON

February 1984   Leeds

FACSIMILE OF

A BOOK OF FRUITS AND FLOWERS

A
BOOK
OF
Fruits & Flovvers.

SHEWING
The Nature and Use of them, either
for Meat or Medicine.

AS ALSO:
**To Preserve, Conserve, Candy, and in Wedges,
or Dry them. To make Powders, Civet bagges,**
all sorts of Sugar-works, turn'd works in Sugar,
Hollow, or Frutages ; and to Pickell them.

And for Meat.
To make Pyes, Biscat, Maid Dishes, Marchpanes, Leeches,
and Snow, Craknels, Caudels, Cakes, Broths, Fritter-
stuffe, Puddings, Tarts, Syrupes, and Sallets.

For Medicines.
To make all sorts of Poultisses, and Serecloaths for any member
swell'd or inflamed, Ointments, Waters for all Wounds, and Cancers, Salves
for Aches, to take the Ague out of any place Burning or Scalding ;
For the stopping of suddain Bleeding, curing the Piles,
Ulcers, Ruptures, Coughs, Consumptions, and killing
of Warts, to dissolve the Stone, killing the
Ring-worme, Emroids, and Dropsie,
Paine in the Ears and Teeth,
Deafnesse.

Contra vim mortis, non est Medicamen in hortis.

LONDON:
Printed by *M. S.* for *Tho: Jenner* at the South entrance of the *Royall
Exchange*, London. 1653.

Of Lemmons.

Lemmon

A Lemmon Sallet.

Ake *Lemmons*, rub them upon a Grate, to make their rinds smooth, cut them in halves, take out the meat of them, and boyle them in faire water a good while, changing the water once or twice in the boyling, to take away the bitternesse of them, when they are tender take them out and scrape away all the meat (if any be left) very cleane, then cut them as thin as you can (to

make

make them hold) in a long ſtring, or in reaſonable ſhort pieces, and lay them in your glaſſe, and boyling ſome of the beſt *White-wine* vineger with ſhugar, to a reaſonable thin Syrupe, powre it upon them into your glaſſe, and keep them for your uſe.

To Preſerve Orenges or Lemmons.

Take your *Oranges* or *Lemmons,* lay them in water three dayes, and three nights, to take away their bitterneſſe, then boyle them in faire water till they be tender, make as much Syrupe for them as will make them ſwim about the pan, let them not boyle too long therein, for it will make the skins tough ; then let them lie all night in the Syrupe, to make them take the Syrupe in the morning, boyle the Syrupe to his thickneſſe, and put them in gally pots or glaſſes, to keep all the yeare, and this is the beſt way to Preſerve *Orenges, Lemmons,* or *Citrons.*

To make Paſt of Lemmons.

Take halfe a dozen of thick-rined *Lemmons,* cut them through the middeſt, and boyle them tender in faire water, then ſtamp them in a Morter, ſtrayne the juyce or pulp from them, and dry it, and put two pound of *Shugar* to it, then make it into what faſhion you will, on a ſheet of white paper, dry it in an Oven, and turne it often for two dayes and two nights, for in that time it will be dry enough ; box it thus up, and it will endure all the Yeare.

Sweet Bagges to lay amongſt Linnen.

Take *Orris, Cypris, Calamus, Fuſis,* all of them groſſe beaten, and *Gallingall* roots, of each a handfull, and as much of the ſmall tops of *Lavender,* dryed, and put them into baggs to lay among your cloaths. You may put in a handfull or two of *Damask Roſe* leaves dryed, which will ſomewhat better the ſent.

Medicines made of Lemmons.

To take away the Spots, or red Pimpels of the face.

Take halfe a pint of raine water, and halfe a pint of good *Verjuice,* ſeeth it till it be halfe conſumed, then whilſt it boils fill it up againe with juyce of *Lemmon,* and ſo let it ſeeth a pretty while ; then take it from the fire, and when it is cold put to it the whites of four new laid Eggs, well beaten, and with this water annoynt the place often.
A very

A very good Medicine for the Stone.

Make a Poſſet of a quart of *Rheniſh* wine, a pint of *Ale*, and a pint of *Milke*, then take away the curd, and put into the drink, two handfulls of *Sorrell*, one handfull of *Burnet*, and halfe a handfull of *Balm*, boyle them together a good while, but not too long, leaſt the drink be too unpleaſant, then take of the drink a quarter of a pint, or rather halfe a pint, at once, at morning, and to bedward, putting therein firſt two or three ſpoonfulls of juice of *Lemmons*, this is an excellent Medicine for the *Stone in the Kidneyes*, to diſſolve and bring it away. It is very good in theſe Diſeaſes of the *Stone*, to uſe *Burnet* often in your drink at Meales, and often to ſteep it in over night, and in the morning put in three or foure ſpoonfulls of juice of *Lemmons*, and to drink thereof a good draught every morning a week together, about the full of the Moone, three dayes before, and three dayes after.

To roſte a Shoulder of Mutton with Lemmons.

Take a Shoulder of *Mutton* halfe roſted, cut off moſt of the meat thereof, in thin ſlices, into a faire diſh with the gravy thereof, put thereto about the quantity of a pint of clarret wine, with a ſpoonfull or two at moſt of the beſt wine *Vineger*, ſeaſon it with *Nutmeggs*, and a little *Ginger*, then pare off the rines of one or two good *Lemmons*, and ſlice them thin into the *Mutton*, when it is almoſt well ſtewed between two diſhes, and ſo let them ſtew togethert wo or three warmes, when they are enough, put them in a clean diſh, and take the ſhoulder blade being well broyled on a grid-iron, and lay it upon your meat, garniſhing your diſhes with ſome ſlices and rinds of the *Lemmons*, and ſo ſerve it.

To Boyle a Capon with Oranges and Lemmons.

Take *Orenges* and *Lemmons* peeled, and cut them the long way, and if you can keep your cloves whole, and put them into your beſt Broth of *Mutton* or *Capon*, with *Prunes* or *Currants* three or four dayes, and when they have been well ſodden, cut whole *Pepper*, great *Maſe*, a great peice of *Suggar*, ſome *Roſe-water*, and either *White* wine, or *Clarret* wine, and let all theſe ſeeth together a while, and ſerve it upon Sopps with your *Capon*.

A Lemmond Sallet.

Cut out ſlices of the peele of the *Lemmons*, long wayes, a quarter

ter of an inch one piece from another, and then flice the *Lemmons* very thin, and lay them in a difh croffe, and the peeles about the *Lemmons*, and fcrape a good deal of *Suggar* upon them, and fo ferve them.

Of Quinces.

The beft way to Preferve Quinces.

FIrft pare and coare the *Quinces*, and boyle them in faire water till they be very tender, not covering them, then taking them out of the water, take to every pound of them, two pound of *Sugar*, and half a pint of water, boyle it to a Syrupe, fcumming it well, then put in fome of the Jelly that is wafhed from the *Quince* kernels, and after that, making it boyle a little, put in your *Quinces*, boyle them very faft, keeping the holes upward as neer as you can, for fear of breaking, and when they are fo tender that yon may thruft a rufh through them, take them off, and put them up in your glaffes, having firft faved fome Syrupe till it be cold to fill up your glaffes.

A fpeciall Remembrance in doing them.

When you Preferve *Quinces*, or make *Marmalade*, take the Kernels out of the raw *Quinces*, and wafh off the Jelly that groweth about them, in faire water, then ftraine the water and Jelly from the kernels, through fome fine Cobweb laune, and put the fame into the *Marmalade*, or preferved *Quinces*, when they are well fcum'd, but put not fo much into your *Quinces*, as into the *Marmalade*, for it will Jelly the Syrupe too much ; put fix or feven fpoonfulls of Syrupe into the Jelly. Before you put it into the *Marmalade*, you muft boyle your *Quinces* more for *Marmalade*, then to preferve your *Quinces*, and leaft of them when you make your clear Cakes.

When you would preferve your *Quinces* white, you muft not cover them in the boyling, and you muft put halfe as much *Sugar* more for the white, as for the other. When you would have them r ed, you muft cover them in the boyling.

To Pickle Quinces.

Boyle your *Quinces* that you intend to keep, whole and unpared,

Quince

in faire water, till they be foft, but not too violently for feare you break them, when they are foft take them out, and boyle fome *Quinces* pared, quarter'd, and coar'd, and the parings of the *Quin*ces with them in the fame liquor, to make it ftrong, and when they have boyled a good time, enough to make the liquor of fufficient ftrength, take out the quartered *Quinces* and parings, and put the liquor into a pot big enough to receive all the *Quin*ces, both whole and quartered, and put them into it, when the liquor is thorow cold, and fo keep them for your ufe clofe covered.

To make Quince Cakes.

Prepare your *Quinces*, and take the juſt weight of them in *Sugar*, beaten finely. and ſearcing halfe of it, then of the reſt make a Syrupe, uſing the ordinary proportion of a pint of water to a pound of *Sugar*, let your *Quinces* be well beaten, and when the Syrupe is cand height, put in your *Quince*, and boyle it to a paſt, keeping it with continuall ſtirring, then work it up with the beaten *Sugar* which you reſerved, and theſe Cakes will taſt well of the *Quinces*.

To make Printed Quidony of Quinces.

Take two pound of *Quinces*, paired, coared, and cut in ſmall pieces, and put them into a faire poſnet, with a quart of faire water, and when they are boyled tender, put into them one pound of *Sugar* clarified, with halfe a pint of faire water, let them boyle till all the fruit fall to the bottom of the poſnet, then let the liquid ſubſtance run through a faire linnen cloath into a clean baſon, then put it into a poſnet, and let it boyle till it come to a jelly, then Print it in your Moulds, and turne it into your boxes. You ſhall know when it is ready to Print, by rouling it on the back of a Spoone.

Of Roſes.

To make ſweet Bagges to lay Linnen in.

Take *Damask Roſe* budds, pluck them, and dry the leaves in the ſhadow, the tops of *Lavender* flowers, ſweet *Margerom*, and *Baſill*, of each a handfull, all dryed and mingled with the *Roſe* leaves, take alſo of *Benjamin*, *Storax*, *Gallingall*-roots, and *Ireos* or *Orris* roots, twice as much of the *Orris* as of any of the other, beaten in fine powder : a peece of cotten wool wetted in *Roſe*-water, and put to it a good quantity of *Musk* and *Ambergreece* made into powder, and ſprinkle them with ſome *Civet* diſſolved in *Roſe*-water, lay the Cotten in double paper, and dry it over a chaffin diſh of coales : Laſtly, take halfe a handfull of *Cloves*, and as much *Cinamon* bruiſed, not ſmall beaten, mixe all theſe together, and put them up in your Bagge.

A very

A very good Poultis for any Member ſwell'd and infla-med, and not broken, to take away the paine.

Take three pints of new milk, of ſtale Manchet crums two hand-fulls, or ſo much as ſhall make the milk ſomewhat thick, and there-to put two handfulls of dryed red *Roſe* leaves, and three ounces of Oyle of *Roſes*, boyle all theſe together to the thickneſſe of a Poul-tiſſe, then let it ſtand and coole, and while it cooleth take a ſpoon-full of Oyle of *Roſes*, and with a warm hand rub the place grieved, till the Oyle be dryed in, and then lay the Poultiſſe as warm as you may endure it, to the part inflamed ; doe this morning and even-ing for three or four dayes, as you ſhall ſee cauſe.

To make a ſweet Cake, and with it a very ſweet water.

Take *Damask Roſe* leaves, *Bay* leaves, *Lavinder* tops, ſweet *Mar-jerome* tops, I *reos* powder, *Damask* powder, and a little *Musk* firſt diſſolved in ſweet water, put the *Roſe* leaves and hearbs into a Ba-ſon, and ſprinkle a quarter of a pint of *Roſe*-water among them, and ſtirring them all together, cover the Baſon cloſe with a diſh, and let them ſtand ſo covered, all night, in the morning Diſtill them, ſo ſhall you have at once an excellent ſweet water, and a very fine ſweet Cake to lay among your fineſt linnen.

Oyle of Roſes.

Take Sallet Oyle and put it into an earthen pot, then take *Roſe* leaves, clip off all the white, and bruiſe them a little, and put them into the Oyle, and then ſtop the top cloſe with paſt, and ſet it into a boyling pot of water, and let it boyle one hour, then let it ſtand al one night upon hot embers, the next day take the Oyle, and ſtraine it from the *Roſe* leaves, into a glaſſe, and put therein ſome freſh *Roſe* leaves, clipt as before, ſtop it, and ſet it in the Sun every day for a fortnight or three weeks.

Syrupe of Roſes.

Take *Damask Roſes*, clip off the white of them, and take ſix ounces of them to every pint of faire water, firſt well boyled and ſcummed, let them ſtand ſo as aboveſaid, twelve hours, as you doe in the Syrupe of *Violets*, wringing out the *Roſes* and putting in new eight times, then wringing out the laſt put in onely the juice of four ounces of *Roſes*, ſo make it up as before, if you will put in

B   *Rubarb,*

Rubarb, take to every two drams, flice it, firing it on a thred, hang it within the pot after the firft fhifting, and let it infufe within your *Rofes*: Some ufe to boyle the *Rubarb* in the Syrupe, but it is dangerous, the Syrupe prgeth *Choller* and *Melancholly*.

A Conferve of Rofes.

Take red *Rofe* buds, clip of all the white, bruifed, and withered from them, then weigh them out, and taking to every pound of *Rofes* three pound of *Sugar*, ftamp the *Rofes* by themfelves very fmall putting a little juice of *Lemmons* or *Rofe* water to them as they wax dry, when you fee the *Rofes* fmall enough, put the *Sugar* to them, and beat them together till they be well mingled, then put it up in Gally pots or glaffes; in like manner are the Conferverves of Flowers, of *Violets, Cowflips, Marigolds, Sage,* and *Sea boife* made.

To Preferve Rofes or any other Flowers.

Take one pound of *Rofes*, three pound of *Sugar*, one pint of *Rofe* water, or more, make your Syrupe firft, and let it ftand till it be cold, then take your *Rofe* leaves, having firft clipt off all the white, put them into the cold Syrupe, then cover them, and fet them on a foft fire, that they may but fimper for two or three hours, then while they are hot put them into pots or glaffes for your ufe.

How to Preferve Barbaries.

Firft take the faireft *Barbaries*, and of them the greateft bunches you can get, and with a needle take out the ftones on the one fide of them, then weigh out to every halfe pound of them one pound of *Sugar*, put them into a Preferving pan, ftrow the *Sugar* on them, and let them boyle a quarter of an hour foftly, then taking out the *Barbaries* let the Syrupe boyle a quarter of an hour more, then put in the *Barbaries* againe, and let them boyle a pretty while with the Syrupe, then take them from the Syrupe, and let them both ftand till they be cold, and fo put them up.

To keep Barbaries to garnifh your Meat.

Take the worft of them, and boyle them in faire water, and ftraine the liquor from them, and while the liquor is hot put it into your *Barbaries*, being clean picked, and ftop them up, and if they

mould

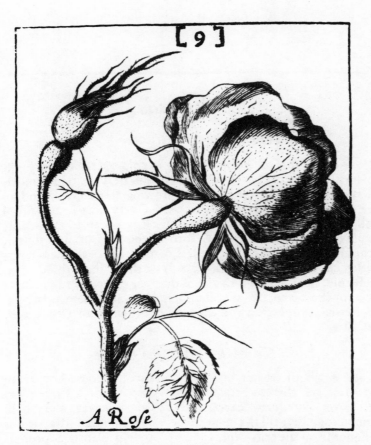

A Rose

mould much, wash them throughly in the liquor, then boyle the
liquor againe, and strayne it, and let it coole, then put it to your
Barbaries againe.

Conserve of Barbaries.

Take your *Barbaries*, pick them clean in faire branches, and
wash them clean, and dry them on a cloath, then take some other
Barbaries, and boyle them in *Claret* wine till they be very soft,
then straine them, and rub them so well through the strainer, that
you may know the substance of them, and boyle up this matter
thus strained out, till it be very sweet, and somwhat thick, then se=
ting it by till it be cold, and then put in your branches of *Barba-*
ries into gally pots, or glasses, and fill it up with the cold Syrupe,
and so shall you have both Syrupe, and also *Barbaries*, to use at
your pleasure.

B 2   Of

Of Almonds.

To make Almond Biscate.

STeepe one pound of *Almonds* so long in cold water, till they will blanch, then put them in *Rose*-water, and beat them in so much *Rose*-water as will keep them from growing to an Oyle, and no more ; take one pound of *Sugar* beaten very fine, and sifted through a Searce, take the whites of six Eggs beat to a froth, as you use to doe for other Bisket, with a spoonfull of fine flower, set the *Almonds* and *Sugar* on a soft Charcoal fire, let them boyle together till they be very thick, and so let them stand till they be almost cold, then beat the Eggs and that together, put in a little *Muske* for the better tast, if you please, then lay them upon papers, in what proportion you will, and dry them in an Oven, with a slack fire.

To make Almond Milke.

Take a rib of *Mutton* or *Veale*, or rather a *Chicken*, boyle it in faire water, put thereto *French Barley*, a *Fennill* root, a *Parsly* root, *Violet* leaves, *Strawberry* leaves, and *Cinquefoyle* leaves, and boyle them all together, till the meat be over boyled, then strayne out the liquor from the rest, while they are boyling blanch a proportion of *Almonds* answerable to the liquor, beat them well in a clean stone Morter, and then grind them therein with *Rose* water and *Sugar*, and when they are well ground put in all your liquor by little and little, and grind with them till they be all well Compounded, and then strayne it into a faire glasse, and use it at your pleasure.

An approved Medicine for the running of the Reines.

Make *Almond* Milke of *Plantine* water, or else boyle *Plantine* in the liquor whereof you make your *Almond* Milk, take a quart of it, and put thereto three spoonfulls of *Lentive farine*, and three spoonfulls of *Cinamon* water, take of this at six in the morning, a good draught, two hours before dinner another, at four of the clock in the afternoon, a third, and two hours after supper a fourth ; and twice or thrice between meals, eat a spoonfull of

Conserve

Conferve of Red *Rofes* at a time.

Oyle of Almonds.

Take *Almonds*, blanch them, and put them into a pot, and fet that pot in another pot of water that boyleth, and the fteam of the feething pot will arife and enter into the pot with the *Almonds*, and that will become Oyle when they are ftamped and wringed through a cloath. Thus they make Oyle of the kernels of *Filberts*, *Walnuts*, &c.

A Barley Cream to procure fleep, or Almond Milke.

Take a good handfull of French *Barley*, wafh it cleane in warme water, and boyle it in a quart of fayre water to the halfe, then put out the water from the *Barley*, and put the *Barley* into a pottell of new clean water, with a *Parfley*, and a *Fennell* root, clean wafhed, and picked with *Bourage*, *Buglos*, *Violet* leaves, and *Lettice*, of each one handfull, boyle them with the *Barley*, till more then halfe be confumed ; then ftrayne out the liquor, and take of blanched *Almonds* a handfull, of the feeds of *Melons*, *Cucumbers*, *Citralls*, and *Gourds*, husked, of each halfe a quarter of an ounce, beat thefe feeds, and the *Almonds* together, in a ftone morter, with fo much *Sugar*, and *Rofe*-water as is fit, and ftrayne them through a cleane cloath into the liquor, and drink thereof at night going to bed, and in the night, if this doth not fufficiently provoke fleep, then make fome more of the fame liquor, and boyle in the fame the heads, or a little of white *Poppey*.

An Oyntment to kill the Worms in little Children.

For ftomach Wormes, annoynt the ftomach with Oyle of *Wormwood*, and the belly with Oyle of fweet *Almonds*, for belly Wormes take all of *Wormwood*, Oyle of *Savine*, and the Powder of *Aloe Cicatrina*, finely beaten, annoynt the belly therewith, morning and evening. You muft not ufe *Savine* in Medicines for Mayden Children, but in ftead of Oyle of *Savine*, take as much of an Oxes Gall.

To make the beft white Puddings.

Take a pound of *Almonds*, blanch them, ftamp them, putting in a little Milk fometime to them in the ftamping, then put to them three handfulls of fine Flower, or as much grated bread firft baked

in

in an Oven, fix Eggs well beaten, a good deale of marrow cut in little pieces, feafon them with *Nutmeg* and *Sugar*, three fpoon-fulls of *Rofe-water*, and a little Salt ; temper them all together, with as much Cream as will ferve to wet or mingle them ; and fo fill them up.

An Almond Candle.

Blanch Jordan *Almonds*, beat them with a little fmall Ale, and ftrayne them out with as much more Ale as you minde to make your Caudle of, then boyle it as you doe an Egg Caudle, with a little Mace in it, and when it is off the fire fweeten it with Sugar.

To make fine white Leach of Almonds.

Take halfe a pound of fmall Almonds, beat them, and ftrayne them with Rofe water, and fweet Milk from the Cow, and put into it two or three pieces of large Mace, one graine of Musk, two ounces of Ifinglaffe, and fo boyle it in a Chafin-difh of coales, a quarter of an hour, till it will ftand, which you fhall try thus, fet a faucer in a little cold water, fo that none come into it, and put a fpoonfull of the Leach into it, and if you fee that ftand, take the other off the fire, then you may flice it in what fafhion you pleafe.

To make Almond Butter.

Blanch one pound of *Almonds*, or more, or leffe, as you pleafe, lay them four hours in cold water, then ftamp them with fome Rofe water, as fine as you can, put them in a cloath, and preffe out as much Milk as you can ; then if you think they be not e-nough beat them, and ftraine them againe, till you get as much Milk of them, as you can ; then fet it on the fire, till they be rea-dy to boyle, putting in a good quantity of Salt and Rofe-water, to turne it after one boyling, being turned, take it off, caft it abroad upon a linnen cloath, being holden between two, then with a fpoon take off the Whey under the cloath, fo long as any will drop or run, then take fo much of the fineft Sugar you can get, as will fweeten it, and melt it in as much Rofe-water as will ferve to diffolve it, put thereto fo much *Saffron* in fine powder, as will co-lou it, and fo fteeping the *Saffron* and *Sugar* in Rofe-water, fea-fon your Butter therewith, when you make it up.

To

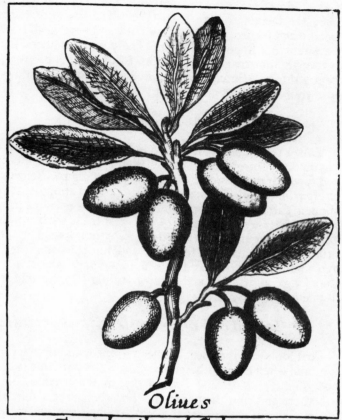

Oliues

To make Almond Cakes.

Take of Jordan Almonds, one pound, beat them as you doe for Almond milk, draw them through a ſtrainer, with the yolks of two or three Eggs, ſeaſon it well with Sugar, and make it into a thick Batter, with fine flower, as you doe for Bisket bread, then powre it on ſmall Trencher plates, and bake them in an Oven, or baking pan, and theſe are the beſt Almond Cakes.

To make Paſte of Almonds.

Take one pound of ſmall Almonds, blanch them out of hot water into cold, then dry them with a cloath, and beat them in a
ſtone

stone Morter, till they come to Past, putting now and then a spoonfull of Rose water to them, to keep them from Oyling, when they are beaten to fine past, take halfe a pound of *Sugar* finely beaten and searsed, put it to your past, and beat it till it will twist between your fingers and thumb, finely without knots, for then it is enough, then make thereof Pyes, Birds, Fruits, Flowers, or any pretty things, printed with Molds, and so gild them, and put them into your Stove, and use them at your pleasure.

To make a Marchpine.

Take a pound of small Almonds, blanch them, and beat them, as you doe your past of Almonds, then drive it into a sheet of past, and spread it on a botome of wafers, according to the proportion, or bignesse you please, then set an edge round about it, as you doe, about a Tart, and pinch it if you will, then bake it in a pan, or O-ven, when it is enough, take it forth, and Ice it with an Ice made of *Rose-water* and Sugar, as thick as batter, spread it on with a brush of bristles, or with feathers, and put it in the Oven againe, and when you see the Ice rise white and dry, take it forth, and stick long comfits in it, and set up a staddard in the middest of it, so gild it, and serve it.

To make White-Broth with Almonds.

First look that the Meat be clean washed, and then set it on the fire, and when it boyleth, scum it clean, and put some salt into the pot, then take *Rosemary, Time, Hysop,* and *Marjerome,* bind them together, and put them into the pot, then take a dish of sweet Butter, and put it also into the pot amongst the meat, and take whole Mase, and bind them in a cloath, and put them into the pot, with a quantity of Verjuice, and after that take such a quan-tity of Almonds as shall serve turne, blanch them, and beat them in the Morter, and then straine them with the broth when your Meat is in, and when these Almonds are strained put them in a pot by themselves, with some *Sugar,* a little *Ginger,* and also a little Rose-water, then stir it while it boyle, and after that take some sli-ced *Oringes* without the kernels, and boyle them with the broth of the pot, upon a chafin-dish of coales, with a little *Sugar,* and then have some Sipits ready in a platter, and serve the meat up-on them, and put not your Almonds in till it be ready to be served.

Of

Straw- *berries*

Of Straw-Berries.

A Tart of Straw-Berries.

PIck and waſh your *Straw-Berries* clean, and put them in the paſt one by another, as thick as you can, then take *Sugar, Cinamon,* and a little *Ginger* finely beaten, and well mingled together, caſt them upon the *Straw Berries,* and cover them with the lid finely cut into Lozenges, and ſo let them bake a quarter of an houre, then take it out, ſtrewing it with a little *Cinamon,* and *Sugar,* and ſo ſerve it.

Of Hartichoakes.

How to make a Hartichoake Pye.

BOyle your *Hartichoakes*, take off all the leaves, pull out all the strings, leaving only the bottoms, then seafon them with *Cinamon*, and *Sugar*, layiug between every *Hartichoake* a good piece of Butter, and when you put your Pye into the Oven, ftick the *Hartichoakes* with flices of *Dates*, and put a quarter of a pint of White-wine into the *Pye*, and when you take it out of the Oven, doe the like againe, with fome butter, and fugar, and Rofe-water, melting the butter upon fome coales, before you put it into the Pye.

To keep Hartichoakes for all the yeare.

The fitteft time is about *Michaelmas*, and then according to the proportion of *Hartichoakes* you will keep, feeth a quantity of water in a pot or pan, feafoning it fo with white falt that it may have a reafonable taft, then put a fit quantity of white falt into the water, and boyle them together, and fcum them well ; then put a good quantity of good *Vineger* to them, to make the liquor fomewhat fharp, and boyle it again, then parboyle your *Hartichoakes* that you mind to keep, in another liquor, take them out of it, and let them coole, then fet your firft liquor againe on the fire to boyle, and fcumming it throughly, let it coole againe ; when it is throughly cold, put it up in fome firkin, or large earthen pot, and put in your *Hartichoakes* to them handfomely, for bruifing them ; then cover them clofe from the aire, and fo keep them to fpend at your pleafure.

To Preferve Hartichoakes.

Heat water fcalding hot firft, then put in your *Hartichoakes*, and fcald them, and take away all the bottomes, and leaves about them, then take *Rofe water* and *Sugar* and boyle them alone a little while, then put the *Hartichoakes* therein, and let them boyle on a foft fire till they be tender enough, let them be covered all the time they boyle, then take them out and put them up for your ufe.

To make a maid diſh of Hartechoakes.

Take your *Hartichoakes* and pare away all the top, even to the Meat, and boyle them in ſweet Broth till they be ſomewhat tender, then take them out, and put them in a diſh, and ſeeth them with *Pepper, Cinamon,* and *Ginger,* then put them in the diſh you mean to bake them in, and put in marrow to them good ſtore, and ſo let them bake, and when they be baked, put in a little *Vineger* and *Butter,* and ſtick three or four leaves of the *Hartichoakes* in the diſh when you ſerve them up, and ſcrape *Sugar* upon the diſh.

OF
MEDICINES.

An Excellent Medicine or Salve for an Ache coming of cold, eaſie to be made by any Countrey Houſewife.

Take of good Neats-foot Oyle, Honey, and new Wax, like quantities, boyle them all well together, then put to them a quarter ſo much of *Aqua vitæ* as was of each of the other, and then ſetting it on the fire, boyle it till it be well incorporated together, then ſpread it upon a piece of thin Leather, or thick linnen cloath, and ſo apply it to the place pained.

To cake the Ague out of any place.

Take *Vervine* and *Black Hemlocke,* of each an handfull, boyle them in a pint of freſh *Butter* till they be ſoft, and begin to parch againe, then ſtraine the *Butter* from the hearbs, and put it into a gally pot, and two or three times annoynt the place grieved with a ſpoonfull or two thereof, *probat.*

For the Ague in Children, or Women with Child.

Take *Venice Terpentine,* ſpread it on the rough ſide of a piece of thin *Leather,* two fingers breadth, and ſtrew thereon the powder of *Frankincenſe* finely beaten, and upon it ſome *Nutmeg* grated, binde

this

this upon the wrifts an hour before the fit comes, and renew it ftill till the fit be gone.

To ftrengthen the Back weak or difeafed.

Take the pith of an Oxes back, wafh it in Wine or Ale, and beating it very fmall ftraine it through a courfe cloath, and make a Caudle of it, with *Muskadine*, or ftrong *Ale*, boyling therein a few *Dates* fliced, and the ftones taken out, and drink it firft and laft as warm as you can, walking well, but temperately after it. Toafted dates often eaten are very good for the fame.

For a Paine or Ache in the Back.

Take *Nepe*, *Archangel*, *Parfley*, and *Clarie*, of each halfe a hand-full, wafh them cleane, and cut them fmall, and then fry them with a little fweet Butter, then take the yolks of three or four Eggs, beat them well together, and put them to the Hearbs, fry them all together, and eat them fafting every morning, with fome *Sugar* ; to take away the unfavorineffe of the Hearbs, fome ufe to take only *Clary* leaves, and *Parfley* wafhed, not cut, or *Clary* leaves alone, and powring the yolks of the Eggs upon them, fo fry them, and eat them.

For a fuddain Bleeding at the Nofe.

Burne an Egg-fhell in the fire till it be as black as a coale, then beate it to fine powder, and let the party fnuffe it up into his Noftrills.

A Medicine for Burning or Scalding.

Take *Madenwort*, ftamp it, and feeth it in frefh Butter, and therewith anoynt the place grieved prefently.

For the Canker in Womens Breafts.

Take *Goofe*-dung, and *Celedonie*, ftamp them well together, and lay it plaifter-wife to the foare, it will cleanfe the *Canker*, kill the wormes, and heale the foare.

For

For the Canker in the Mouth.

Take the juice of *Plantaine*, *Vineger*, and *Rose* water, of each a like quantity, mingle them together, and wash the mouth often with them.

To make a Tooth fall out of it selfe.

Take wheat flower and mix it with the Milk of an Hearb called *Spurge*, make thereof a past, and fill the hole of the Tooth therewith, and leave it there, changing it every two houres, and the Tooth will fall out.

To take away the cause of the paine in the Teeth.

Wash the mouth two or three times together in the morning every moneth, with *White-wine* wherein the root of *Spurge* hath been sodden, and you shall never have paine in your Teeth.

For a Consumption.

Take Ash-keyes so soon as they look wither'd, set them into an Oven, the bread being drawne, in a pewter, or rather an earthen dish, and being so dryed pull off the out side, and reserving the inner part, of the seed, or keyes, beat them to fine powder, and either mix it with good English honey, and so eat of it, first and last, morning and evening, a pretty deale of it at once, upon the point of a knife, or else drink of the powder in some posset Ale, or thin broth. Mares milk, or Asses milk, which is best, being drunk warm morning and evening, is the most soveraigne Medicine for it.

An excellent Medicine for the Cough of the Lungs.

Take *Fennell* and *Angelica* of each one handfull, the leaves in Summer, roots in Winter, sliced figgs twelve, but if the body be bound, twenty at least ; green Licorice if you can, two or three good sticks scraped and sliced, Anniseed cleaved and bruised, two good spoonfulls, two or three Parsley roots scraped, and the pith taken out, and twenty leaves of Foale-foot, boyle all these in three pints of *Hysop* water, to a pint and halfe, then straine it out into a glasse, putting to it as much white *Sugar*-candy as will make it sweet, drink hereof, being warmed, five spoonfulls at a time, first in the morning, and last in the evening, taking heed that you eat nor drink any thing two howres before nor after.

Of

Of Violets.

The use of Oyle of Violets.

OYle of *Violets, Cammomile, Lillies, Elder flowers, Cowslips, Rue, Wormwood,* and *Mint,* are made after the same sort ; Oyle of *Violets,* if it be rubbed about the Tempels of the head, doth remove the extream heat, affwageth the head Ache, provoketh sleep, and moistneth the braine ; it is good against melancholly, dullnesse, and heavinesse of the spirits, and against swellings, and soares that be over-hot.

The Syrupe of Violets.

Take faire water, boyle it, scum it, and to every ounce of it so boyled and scummed, take six ounces of the blew of *Violets,* only shift them as before, nine times, and the last time take nine ounces of *Violets,* let them stand between times of shifting, 12 houres, keeping the liquor still on hot embers, that it may be milk warm, and no warmer ; after the first shifting you must stamp and straine your last nine ounces of *Violets,* and put in only the juice of them, then take to every pint of this liquor thus prepared, one pound of *Sugar* finely beaten, boyle it, and keep it with stirring till the *Sugar* be all melted, which if you can, let be done before it boyle, and then boyle it up with a quick fire. This doth coole and open in a burning *Ague,* being dissolved in *Almond* milk, and taken ; especially it is good for any Inflamation in Children. The Conserves are of the same effect.

The use of Conserve of Violets and Cowslips.

That of *Cowslips* doth marveloufly strengthen the Braine, preserveth against Madnesse, against the decay of memory, stoppeth Head-ache, and most infirmities thereof ; for *Violets* it hath the same use the Syrupe hath.

To

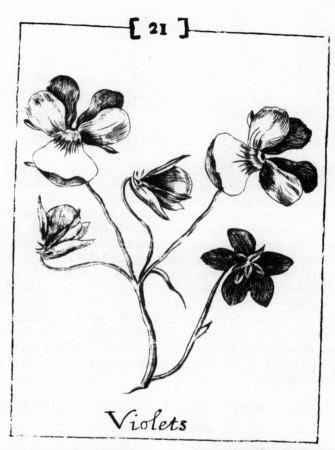

Violets

To make Paste of Violets, or any kind of Flowers.

Take your Flowers, pick them, and ſtamp them in an *Alablaſter* morter, then ſteep them two howres in a ſauſer of *Roſe*-water, after ſtraine it, and ſteep a little *Gum Dragon* in the ſame water, then beat it to paſt, print it in your Moulds, and it will be of the very colour and taſt of the Flowers, then gild them, and ſo you may have every Flower in his owne colour, and taſt better for the mouth, then any printed colour.

Powder of Violets.

Take ſweet *Ireos* roots one ounce, red *Roſes* two ounces, *Storax* one ounce and a halfe, *Cloves* two drams, *Marjerome* one dram, *Lavinder* flowers one dram and a halfe, make theſe into powder;
then

then take eight graines of fine *Muske* powdered, alſo put to it two ounces of *Roſe*-water, ſtir them together, and put all the reſt to them, and ſtir them halfe an hour, till the water be dryed, then ſet it by one day, and dry it by the fire halfe an houre, and when it is dry put it up into bagges.

A good Plaiſter for the Strangury.

Take *Violets*, and *Hollyhokes*, and *Mercury*, the leaves of theſe Hearbs, or the ſeeds of them, alſo the rinde of the *Elderne* tree, and *Leydwort*, of each of theſe a handfull, and beat them ſmall, and ſeeth them in water, till halfe be conſumed, and put thereto a little oyle Olive, and make thereof a plaiſter, and lay it to the ſoare and reines ; alſo in the ſummer thou muſt make him a drink on this manner, take *Saxifrage*, and the leaves of *Elderne*, five leav'd graſſe, and ſeath them in a pottell of ſtaile Ale, till the halfe be waſted, then ſtraine it, and keep it clean, and let the ſick drink thereof firſt and laſt, and if you lack theſe hearbs becauſe of winter, then take the roots of five-leav'd graſſe, and dry them, and make thereof a powder, then take Oyſter-ſhells, and burne them, and make powder alſo of them, and mingling them toge-ther, let the ſick uſe thereof in his pottage, and drink, and it will help him.

A Medicine for ſore blood-ſhotten, and Rhue-matick eyes.

Take ground *Ivy*, *Daiſes*, and *Celedony*, of each a like quantity, ſtamp and ſtraine out the juice out of them, and put to it a little brown *Sugar* Candy diſſolved in white Roſe-water, and drop two or three drops of this liquor at one time into the grieved eye, with a feather, lying upon the back when you doe it an hour after, this is a moſt approved Medicine to take away all *Inflamations*, *Spots*, *Webbs*, *Itches*, *Smartings*, or any griefe whatſoever in the eyes.

A Gliſter to open and looſen the Body being bound, which may ſafely be admini-ſtred to any man or woman.

Take *Mallowes* and *Mercury* unwaſhed, of each two handfulls, halfe a handſull of *Barley* clean rubbed and waſhed, boyle them in

a pottell of running water to a quart, then ſtrayne out the water,
and put it in a Skillet, and put to it three ſpoonfulls of Sallet
Oyle, and two ſpoonfulls of Honey, and a little ſalt ; then make
it luke warm, and ſo miniſter it.

To cleanſe the head, and take the Ache away.

Chew the root of *Pellitory of Spaine,* often in the mouth.

A Medicine that hath healed old Sores upon the leggs, that have run ſo long that the bones have been ſeen.

Take a quantity of good ſweet *Cream,* and as much *Brimſtone*
beaten in fine powder, as will make it thick like Paſte, then
take ſo much *Butter* as will make it into the form of Oyntment,
and herewith annoynt the place grieved, twice a day.

An Oyntment for a Rupture.

Take of *Sanicle* two handſulls, of *Adders* tongue, *Doves* foot, and
Shephards purſe, of each as much, of *Limaria* one handfull, chop
them ſomewhat ſmall, and boyle them in *Deers* ſeuet, untill the
Hearbs doe crumble, and wax dry.

A Barley Water to purge the Lungs and lights of all Diſeaſes.

Take halfe a pound of faire *Barley,* a gallon of running water,
Licorice halfe an ounce, *Fennell* ſeed, *Violet* leaves, *Parſley* ſeed, of
each one quarter of an ounce, red *Roſes* as much, *Hyſop* and *Sage*
dryed, a good quantity of either, *Harts tongue* twelve leaves, a
quarter of a pound of *Figges,* and as many *Raiſons,* ſtill the *Figges*
and *Raiſons,* put them all into a new earthen pot, with the water
cold, let them ſeeth well, and then ſtrain the cleareſt from it,
drink of this a good quantity, morning and afternoone, obſerving
good diet upon it, it taketh away all *Agues* that come of heat, and
all ill heat ; it purgeth the *Lights, Spleene, Kidneyes,* and *Bladder.*

To Cure the Diſeaſes of the Mother.

Take ſix or ſeaven drops of the Spirit of *Caſtoreum,* in the begin-
D   ning

ting of the fit, in two or three spoonfulls of posset *Ale,* applying a Plaifter of *Gavanum* to the Navill.

To kill Warts : an approved Medicine.

Take a *Radish* root, scrape off the out-side of it, and rub it all over with salt, then set it thus dressed upright in a saucer, or some other small dish, that you may save the liquor that runneth from it, and therewith annoynt your Warts three or four times in a day, the oftner the better, and in five or six dayes they will consume away, *Sepe probatum.*

For the Piles.

Set a Chafin-dish of coales under a close stoole chaire, or in a close-stoole case, and strew *Amber* beaten in fine powder, upon the coales, and sit downe over it, that the smoak may ascend up into the place grieved.

A Medicine for the Piles.

Take a little *Orpine, Hackdagger,* and *Elecampane,* stamp them all together with *Boares* grease, into the form of an Oyntment, and lay them to the place grieved.

A Diet for the Patient that hath Ulcers or Wounds that will hardly be Cured with Oyntments, Salves, or Plaifters.

Take one pound of *Guaicum,* boyle it in three pottels of *Ale,* with a soft fire, to the consuming of two parts, but if it be where you may have wild Whay, or cheese Whay, they are better. Let the Patient drink of this morning and evening, halfe a pint at a time, and let him sweat after it two hours. His drink at his Meals must be thus used, put into the same vessel where the former was made, to the *Guaicum* that is left, three pottels of *Ale,* and not *Whey,* let it boyle to the one halfe, let him drink thereof at all times, and at his meale, which must be but one in a day, and that so little, that he may rise hungry. Thus he must doe for five dayes together, but he must first be purged.

Of

C ow ſlips

Of Cowſlips.

Oyle of Cowſlips.

OYle of *Cowſlips*, if the Nape of the Neck be annointed with it, is good for the *Palſie*, it comforteth the ſinews, the heart and the head.

The uſe of the Oyle of Wormwood, and Oyle of Mint.

Oyle of *Wormwood* is good for ſtraines and bruiſes, and to comfort the ſtomach ; it is made of the green Hearb, as are the Oyle

of

of *Cammomile, Rue,* and *Mint,* are made.

Oyle of *Mint* comforteth the ftomack, overlayed or weakned with Cafting, it doth drive back, or dry up Weomend breafts, and doth keep them from being foare, being therewith annointed.

Syrupe of Cowflips.

Inftead of running water you muft take diftilled water of *Cow-flips,* put thereto your *Cowflip* flowers clean picked, and the green knobs in the bottome cut off, and therewith boyle up a Syrupe, as in the Syrupe of *Rofes* is fhewed ; it is good againft the *Frenfie,* comforting and ftaying the head in all hot *Agues, &c.* It is good againft the *Palfie,* and procures a fick Patient to fleep ; it muft be taken in *Almond-*milk, or fome other warm thing.

To keep Cowflips for Salates.

Take a quart of *White wine* Vineger, and halfe a quarter of a pound of fine beaten *Sugar,* and mix them together, then take your *Cowflips,* pull them out of the podds, and cut off the green knobs at the lower end, put them into the pot or glaffe wherein you mind to keep them, and well fhaking the *Vineger* and *Sugar* together in the glaffe wherein they were before, powre it upon the *Cowflips,* and fo ftirring them morning and evening to make them fettle for three weeks, keep them for your ufe.

To Conferve Cowflips.

Gather your Flowers in the midft of the day when all the dew is off, then cut off all the white leaving none but the yellow blof-fome fo picked and cut, before they wither, weigh out ten oun-ces, taking to every ten ounces of them, or greater proportion, if you pleafe, eight ounces of the beft refined *Sugar,* in fine powder, put the *Sugar* into a pan, and candy it, with as little water as you can, then taking it off the fire, put in your Flowers by little and little, never ceafing to ftir them till they be dry, and enough ; then put them into glaffes, or gally pots, and keep them dry for your ufe. Thefe are rather Candied then Conferved *Cowflips.*

To Preferve all kinde of Flowers in the Spa-nifh Candy in Wedges.

Take *Violets, Cowflips,* or any other kinde of Flowers, pick
them,

them, and temper them with the pap of two roasted *Apples*, and a drop or two of *Verjuice*, and a graine of *Muske*, then take halfe a pound of fine hard *Sugar*, boyle it to the height of *Manus Christi*, then mix them together, and pour it on a wet Pye plate, then cut it in Wedges before it be through cold, gild it, and so you may box it, and keep it all the year. It is a fine sort of Banquetting stuffe, and newly used, your *Manus Christi* must boyle a good while, and be kept with good stirring.

A Medicine to break and heale sore breasts of VVomen, used by Mid-wives, and other skillfull VVomen in London.

Boyle *Oatmeale*, of the smallest you can get, and red *Sage* together, in running or Conduict water, till it be thick enough to make a Plaister, and then put into it a fit proportion of *Honey*, and let it boyle a little together, take it off the fire, and while it is yet boyling hot, put thereto so much of the best *Venice Terpentine* as will make it thick enough to spread, then spreading it on some soft leather, or a good thick linnen cloath, apply it to the brest, and it will first break the soare, and after that being continued, will also heale it up.

A Medicine that hath recovered some from the Dropsie, whome the Physitian hath given over.

Take green *Broome* and burne it in some clean place, that you may save the ashes of it, take some ten or twelve spoonfulls of the same Ashes, and boyle them in a pint of *White* wine till the vertue of it be in the wine, then coole it, and drayne the wine from the dreggs, and make three draughts of the Wine, and drink one fasting in the morning, another at three in the afternoone, another latt at night neer going to bed. Continue this, and by Gods grace it will cure you.

An especiall Medicine for all manner of Poysson.

Take *Hemp seed*, dry it very well, and get off the husks, and beat the *Hemp seed* into fine powder, take *Mintes* also, dry them, and

and make them into powder, boyle a spoonfull of either of these in halfe a pint of *Goats* milk, a pretty while, then put the milk into a cup to coole, and put into it a spoonfull of *Treacle*, and stir them together till it be coole enough, then drink it in the morning fasting, and eat nothing till noon, or at least two hours ; doe the like at night, and use it so three dayes, and it will kill and overcome any poyson.

Doctor Lewin's *Unguentum Rosatum,* good for the heat in the Back.

Take a certain quantity of *Barrowes* grease, Oyle of sweet *Almonds,* and *Rose-water,* either red or damask, of each a like quantity, but of neither so much as of the *Hoggs* grease, beat them together to an Oyntment, put it in some gally pot, and when you would use it, heat it, and therewith annoynt the Back and Reins.

Of Beanes.

To defend Humours.

TAke *Beanes,* the rinde or the upper skin being pul'd off, bruise them, and mingle them with the white of an Egg, and make it stick to the temples, it keepeth back humours flowing to the Eyes.

To dissolve the Stone, which is one of the Physitians greatest secrets.

Take a peck of green *Beane* cods, well cleaved, and without dew or rain, and two good handfulls of *Saxifrage,* lay the same into a Still, one row of *Bean* cods, another of *Saxifrage,* and so Distill another quart of water after this manner, and then Distill another proportion of *Bean* codds alone, and use to drink oft these two Waters ; if the Patient be most troubled with heat of the Reins, then it is good to use the *Bean* codd water stilled alone more often, and the other upon comming downe of the sharp gravell or stone.

Unguentum Sanativum.

Take of *Terpentine* one pound, *Wax* six ounces, Oyle of *Cammomile*

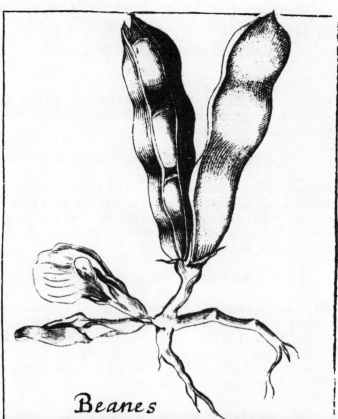

Beanes

mile halfe a pint, put all thefe together in a pan, and put to them
a handfull of *Cammomile*, bruifed, or cut very fmall, boyle them
upon a foft fire till they be well melted, and no more ; then take
it from the fire, and ftrayne it into a clean pan, and fo let it coole
all night, and in the morning put it up for your ufe.   This Oyntment is good for any cut, wound, or breaking of the flefh, it eat-
eth away dead flefh, and ranklings, and doth heale againe quickly.

A Serecloath for all Aches.

Take *Roffen* one pound, *Perroffen* a quarter of a pound, as *Maftick* and *Deer fewet* the like, *Turpentine* two ounces, *Cloves* bruifed,
one ounce, *Mace* bruifed, two ounces, *Saffron* two drams, boyle
all thefe together in Oyle of *Cammomile*, and keep it for your ufe.

An

An Oyntment to be made at any time of the yeare, and is approved good, and hath helped old Paines, Griefes, and Aches.

Take *Steers Gall, Sallet Oyle*, and *Aqua vitæ*, of each five spoonfulls, boyle them together a little, and therewith annoint the place pained, by the fire, and lay a warm cloath on it.

An Oyntment for the Sciatica.

Roaste a handfull or two of *Onions*, and take *Neats-foot* Oyle, and *Aqua vitæ*, of each a pint, stamp, or rather boyle all these together to an Oyle, or Oyntment, and straine it into a gally pot, and therewith annoynt the place grieved as hot as you can endure it, morning and evening.

A VVater to drive away any Infection.

Take *Draggons, Angelica, Rue, Wormwood*, of each a handfull, chop them pretty small, and steep them in a quart of *White-wine*, twenty four hours, then distill them in a Still, and reserve the water in a glasse close stopped ; give to the sick Patient six or seaven spoonfuls thereof at a time fasting, and let him fast an houre and an halfe after, and keep himselfe very warme in his bed, or otherwise.

An excellent Conservative for the stomach, helping digestion, warming the braine, and drying the Rheumes.

Take two ounces of good old Conserve of red *Roses*, of chosen *Methridate* two drams, mingle ihem well together, and eat thereof to bed-ward, the quantity of a hazell nut ; this doth expell all windinesse of the stomach, expelleth raw humours and venomous vapours, causeth good digestion, dryeth the Rheume, strengthneth the memory and sight.

An

An Oyntment for any wound or sore.

Take two pound of *Sheeps* suet, or rather *Deers* suet, a pint of *Candy Oyle*, a quarter of a pound of the newest and best *Bees-wax*, melt them together, stirring them well, and put to them one ounce of the Oyle of *Spike*, and halfe an ounce of the *Goldsmiths Boras*, then heating them againe, and stirring them all together, put it up in a gally pot, and keep it close stopped till you have cause to use it ; this is an approved Oyntment to cure any wounds or sores new or old.

An excellent Oyntment for any Bruise or Ache.

Take two pound of *May Butter* purified, powre it out from the dregs, and put to it of *Broome* flowers and *Elder* flowers, of each a good handfull, so clean picked that you use nothing but the leaves, mix them all together in a stone pot, and boyle them seaven or eight howres in a kettell of water, being covered with a board, and kept downe with weights, keeping the kettell alwayes full of water, with the help of another kettell of boyling water ready to fill up the first as it wasteth, and when it waxeth somewhat coole, but not cold, straine the Oyntment from the Hearbs, into a gally pot, and keep it for your use.

A Plaister for a Bile or Push.

Take a yolk of an Egg, and halfe a spoonfull of English *Honey*, mix them together with fine wheat flower, and making it to a Plaister, apply it warme to the place grieved.

An approved good drink for the Pestilence.

Take six spoonfuls of *Draggon*-water, two good spoonfulls of *Wine-Vineger*, two penny weights of English *Saffron*, and as much Treacle of *Gene*, as a little *Walnut*, dissolve all these together upon the fire, and let the Patient drink it blood-warm, within twenty hours or sooner that he is sick, and let him neither eat nor drink six howres after, but lye so warme in his bed, that he may sweat, this expelleth the Disease from the heart, and if he be disposed to a sore, it wlil stteightwayes appeare, which you shall draw out with a Plaister of *Flos Unguentorum*.

E   For

For the Rheume in the gums or teeth.

Boyle *Rosemary* in faire water, with some ten or twelve *Cloves*, shut, and when it is boyled take as much *Clarret* wine as there is water left, and mingle with it, and make it boyle but a little againe, then strayne it into some glasse, and wash the mouth there with morning and evening; this will take away the Rheume in short time; and if you boyle a little *Mastick* therewith, it is the better.

For the Emroids.

Take *Egremony* and bruise it small, and then fry it with *Sheep suet*, and *Honey*, of each a like quantity, and lay it as hot as you can suffer it to the Fundament, and it will heale very faire and well.

An approved medicine for the Dropsey.

Take the Hearb called *Bitter sweet*, it grows in waters, and bears a purple flower, slice the stalks, and boyle a pretty deale of them in *White-wine*, drink thereof first and last, morning and evening, and it will cure the *Dropsey*.

A Powder for Wounds.

Take *Orpiment*, and *Verdigreese*, of each an ounce, of *Vitriall* burned till it be red, two ounces, beat each of them by it selfe in a brasen Morter, as small as flower, then mingle them all together, that they appear all as one, and keep it in bagges of leather, well bound, for it will last seaven years with the same vertue, and it is called *Powder peerlesse*, it hath no peer for working in *Chyrurgery*, for put of this powder in a wound where is dead flesh, and lay scrap't lint about it, and a Plainer of Disklosions next upon it, and it will heale it.

An approved Medicine for the Green sicknesse.

Take a quart of *Clarret* wine, one pound of *Currants*, and a handfull of young *Rosemary* crops, and halfe an ounce of *Mace*, seeth these to a pint, and let the Patient drink thereof three spoonfulls at a time, morning and evening, and eat some of the *Currants* also after.

A Me-

A Medicine for a Pleurisie, Stitch, or Winde, offending in any part of the Body.

Gather the young shutes of *Oake*, after the fall of a *Wood*, and picking out the tenderest and softest of them, especially those which look redest, bind them up together in a wet paper, and roste them in hot embers, as you doe a *Warden*, whereby they will dry to powder, of which powder let the Patient take a spoonfull in a little Posset *Ale*, or *Beer*, warmed, in the morning, fasting after it two hours, or more, if he be able, doing the like about three after noon, and two hours after supper, four or five dayes together, which thus done in the beginning of the Disease, is by often experiments found to cure such windy paines in the side, stomach, or other parts of the body; you may dry them also in a dish, in an Oven after the bread is drawn; you shall doe well to gather enough of them in the Spring, and make good store of the powder then, to keep for all the year following.

An approved Medicine for the Gout in the feet.

Take an *Oxes* paunch new killed, and warm out of the belly, about the latter end of *May*, or beginning of *June*, make two holes therein, and put in your feet, and lay store of warm aloaths about it, to keep it warm so long as can be. Use this three or four dayes together, for three weeks or a moneth, whether you have the fit or paine of the *Gout*, at that time or no, so you have had it at any time before. This hath cured divers persons, that they have never been troubled with it againe.

For one that cannot make water.

Take the white strings of *Filmy* roots, of *Primroses*, wash them very clean, and boyle of them halfe a handfull, in a pint of *Beer* or *White-wine*, till halfe be consumed, then straine it through a clean cloath, and drink thereof a quarter of a pint, somewhat warme, morning and evening, for three dayes, it will purge away all viscous or obstructions stopping the passage of the water, *probatum*.

To kill the Ring worme, and heat thereof.

Take a quart of *White wine* vineger, boyle therein of *Woodbine* leaves, *Sage*, and *Plantaine* of each one handfull, of white *Coperas*, one pound, of *Allum* as much as an Egge; when it is boyled to

halfe

halfe a pint, ſtraine out the liquor, and therewith waſh the ſoare as hard as you can ſuffer it.

To make a Water for all VVounds and Cankers.

Take a handfull of red *Sage* leaves, a handfull of *Selandine*, as much *Woodbine* leaves, then take a gallon of Conduiƈt water, and put the hearbs in it, and let them boyle to a pottell, and then ſtrayning the Hearbs through a ſtrainer, take the liquor and ſet it over the fire againe, and take a pint of Engliſh *Honey*, a good handfull of *Roche Allum*, as much of white *Copperas* tinne beaten, a penny worth of *Graines* bruiſed, and let them boyle all together three or four warms, and then let the ſcum be taken off with a feather, and when it is cold put it in an earthen pot or bottell, ſo as it may be kept cloſe ; and for an old Wound take of the thinneſt, and for a green Wound, of the thickeſt, and having dreſſed them with this Water, cover the ſoare either with *Veale*, or *Mutton*, and skin it with *Dock* leaves.

For a Swelling that cometh ſuddenly in mans Limbs.

Take *Harts* tongue, *Cherſoyle*, and cut them ſmall, and then take dreggs of *Ale*, and *Wheat* Branne, and *Sheeps* tallow molten, and doe all in a pot, and ſeeth them till they be thick, and then make a Plaiſter, and lay it to the ſwelling.

Of Apricocks.

To dry Apricocks.

TAke them when they be ripe, ſtone them, and pare off their rindes very thin, then take halfe as much *Sugar* as they weigh, finely beaten, and lay them with that *Sugar* into a ſilver or earthen diſh, laying firſt a lay of *Sugar*, and then of Fruit, and let them ſtand ſo all night, and in the morning the *Sugar* will be all melted, then put them into a Skillet, and boyle them apace, ſcumming them well, and as ſoon as they grow tender take them off from the fire, and let them ſtand two dayes in the Syrupe, then take them out,

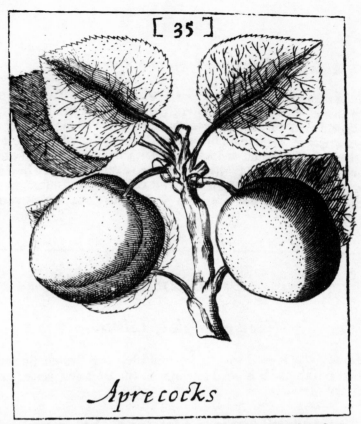

Aprecocks

out, and lay them on a fine plate, and so dry them in a Stove.

Clear Cakes of *Quinces,* or Apricocks.

Take of the beſt *Sugar* finely beaten and ſearced, one pound, to a pound of *Quinces,* or *Apricocks,* ſet your *Sugar* upon a chafin-diſh of coales, and dry it above halfe an houre, then cooling it, ſtir into it a little *Musk* and *Ambergreeſe* finely beaten, and powdered, then pare your *Quinces,* and boyle them in faire water whole, till they be tender, and not covering them for ſo they will be white ; then take them, and ſcrape off all the *Quince* to the coare, into a ſilver diſh, and boyle it therein till it grow dry, which you ſhall perceive by the riſing of it up, when it is thus well dryed, take it off, let it coole, and ſtrew on the *Sugar,* letting ſome other to ſtrew it, till it be all throughly wrought in, then lay it out on glaſſes, plates, or prints of Flowers, or letters, an inch thick, or leſſe as you pleaſe.

The

The best way to Preserve Apricocks.

Take the weight of your *Apricocks*, what quantity foever you mind to ufe, in *Sugar* finely beaten, pare and ftone the *Apricocks*, and lay them in the *Sugar*, in your preferving pan all night, and in the morniug fet them upon hot embers till the *Sugar* be all melted, then let them ftand, and fcald an hour, then take them off the fire, and let them ftand in that Syrupe two dayes, and then boyle them foftly till they be tender and well coloured, and after that when they be cold put them up in glaffes or pots, which you pleafe.

Of Lillies.

The ufe of Oyle of Lillies.

OYle of *Lillies* is good to fupple, mollifie, and ftretch finews that be fhrunk, it is good to annoynt the fides and veines in the fits of the *Stone*.

To Candy all kinde of Flowers as they grow, with their ftalks on.

Take the Flowers, and cut the ftalks fomewhat fhort, then take one pound of the whiteft and hardeft *Sugar* you can get, put to it eight fpoonfulls of *Rofe* water, and boyle it till it will roule between your fingers and your thumb, then take it from the fire, coole it with a ftick, and as it waxeth cold, dip in all your Flowers, and taking them out againe fuddenly, lay them one by one on the bottome of a Sive ; then turne a joyned ftoole with the feet upwards, fet the five on the feet thereof, cover it with a faire linnen cloath, and fet a chafin-difh of coales in the middeft of the ftoole underneath the five, and the heat thereof will run up to the five, and dry your Candy prefently ; then box them up, and they will keep all the year, and look very pleafantly.

To

To make the Rock Candies upon all Spices, Flowers, aud Roots.

Take two pound of *Barbary Sugar*, Clarifie it with a pint of water, and the whites of two *Eggs*, then boyle it in a posnet to the height of *Manus Christi*, then put it into an earthen Pipkin, and therewith the things that you will Candy, as *Cinamon, Ginger, Nutmegs, Rose buds, Marigolds, Eringo roots, &c.* cover it, and stop it close with clay or paste, then put it into a Still, with a leasurely fire under it, for the space of three dayes and three nights, then open the pot, and if the Candy begin to come, keep it unstopped for the space of three or four dayes more, and then leaving the Syrupe, take out the Candy, lay it on a Wyer grate, and put it in an Oven after the bread is drawne, and there let it remaine one night, and your Candy will dry. This is the best way for rock Candy, making so small a quantity.

The Candy Sucket for green Ginger, Lettice, Flowers.

Whatsoever you have Preserved, either Hearbs, Fruits, or Flowers, take them out of the Syrupe, and wash them in warm water, and dry them well, then boyle the *Sugar* to the height of Candy, for Flowers, and draw them through it, then lay them on the bottome of a Sive, dry them before the fire, and when they are enough, box them for your use. This is that the *Comfet-makers* use and call *Sucket Candy*.

Of Grapes.

Syrupe Gresta, or a Syrupe of Unripe Grapes.

Take a good basket full of unripe *Grapes*, set them three dayes in a vessel after they be gathered, stamp them, and straine out the juice out of them, take thereof six quarts, boyle it with a soft fire till the third part be consumed, then four quarts will remaine, let that run through a woollen bagge, and stand till it be
clear

clear in it felfe, then take of the cleareft of it, feven pints, put
thereto five pound of Clarified *Sugar*, boyle them together to the
thickneffe of a Syrupe, and keep it in a glaffe ; it is good for a
perbreaking ftomach, proceeding of Choller, and for a fwelling
ftomach, it taketh away thirft and dryneffe, and chollerick *Agues*,
it is of great comfort to the ftomach of Women being with child,
it is a prefervative againft all manner of Venome, and againft the
Peftilence.

OF
PURGES.

A Purge to drive out the French Pox, before you ufe the Oyntment.

Take halfe a pint of good *Aqua vitæ*, one ounce of *Treacle* of
Gene, one quarter of an ounce of *Sperma cati*, boyle all thefe together on a foft fire halfe a quarter of an hour, and let the Patient
drink this as warme as he can, and lye downe in his bed, and
fweat, and if any of the Difeafe be in his body, this will bring it
forth, and bring him to an eafie loofneffe ; this is thought the
beft and fureft of all other Cures for this infirmity.

The Oyntment for the French Pox.

Take *Barrowes* greafe well tryed from the filmes, beat it in a
Morter till it be fmall and fine, put thereto of *Lethargy* one ounce,
of *Maftick* in fine powder, two ounces, of *Olibanum* in powder, one
ounce, of Oyle of *Spike* one ounce, Oyle of *Paliolum* one ounce,
of *Terpentine* one quarter of a pound , beat all thefe together into
a perfect Oyntment, and therewith annoynt thefe places.

What place to annoynt for the French Pox.

The principall bone in the Nape of the Neck, without the
fhoulder places, taking heed it come not neer the channell bone,
for then it will make the throat fwell, elfe not, the elbowes on
both

both sides, the hip bones, the share, the knees, the hammes, and
the ankles ; if the Patient have no Ache, annoynt not these places, but only the sores till they be whole ; if there be any knobs
lying in the flesh, as many have, annoynt them often, and lay
lint upon them, and brown paper upon the lint, and keep the Patient close out of the aire, and this used will make him whole in
ten dayes by the grace of God.

For a paine in the ears, or deafnesse.

Take a hot loafe, of the bignesse of a Bakers penny loaf, and
pull or cut it in two in the middest, and lay the middle of the
crummy side to the middest, or to the hole of the ear, or ears
pained, as hot as they may be endured, and so bind them fast together on all night, and then if you find any pain in either or both
ears, or any noyse, put into the pained ear or ears, a drop of *Aqua
vitæ*, in each, and then againe binding more hot bread to them,
walk a little while, and after goe to bed ; this done three or four
dayes together, hath taken away the paine, hearing noyse in the
ears, and much eased the deafnesse, and dullnesse of and in many.

Of Marigolds.

A very good Plaister to heale and dry up
a Sore or Cut suddenly.

Take of *Marigold* leaves, *Porret* blades or leaves, and *Housleke*,
of all two handfulls, beat them all very small in a Morter, and
put to them the whites of two new layd Eggs, and beat them very well till they be throughly incorporated with the Eggs, and
apply this till you be well, renew it every day.

The use of Conserve of Marigolds.

Conserve of *Marigolds* taken fasting in the morning, is good
for Melancholy, cureth the trembling and shaking of the heart,
is good to be used against the Plague, and Corruption of the
Aire.

F   *Of*

Of Cherries.

A way to dry Cherries.

Take three quarters of a pound of *Sugar*, and a pound of *Cherries*, their ftalks and ftones taken from them, then put a fpoonfull of clean water in the Skillet, and fo lay a lay of *Cherries* and another of *Sugar*, till your quantity be out, then fet them on the fire, and boyle them as faft as conveniently you can, now and then fhaking them about the Skillet, for fear of burning, and when you think they are enough, and clear, then take them off the fire, and let them ftand till they be halfe cold, then take them out as clear from the Syrupe as you can, and lay them one by one upon fheets of glaffe, fetting them either abroad in the funne, or in a window where the funne may continually be upon them. If they dry not fo faft as you would have them, then in the turning fcrape fome loafe *Sugar* finely upon them, but add no greater heat then the funne will afford, which will be fufficient if they be well tended, and let no dew fall on them by any means, but in the evening fet them in fome warm Cupboard.

How to Preferve Cherries.

Take the *Cherries* when they be new gathered off the Tree, being full ripe, put them to the bottome of your Preferving pan, weighing to every pound of *Cherries*, one pound of *fugar*, then throw fome of the *fugar* upon the *Cherries*, and fet them on a very quick fire, and as they boyle throw on the reft of the *fugar*, till the Syrupe be thick enough, then take them out, and put them in a gally pot while they are warm ; you may if you will, put two or three fpoonfulls of *Rofe-water* to them:

To make all manner of Fruit Tarts.

You muft boyle your Fruit, whether it be *Apple*, *Cherry*, *Peach*, *Damfon*, *Peare*, *Mulberry*, or *Codling*, in faire water, and when they be boyled enough, put them into a bowle, and bruife them with a ladle, and when they be cold ftraine them, and put in red wine, or

C larret

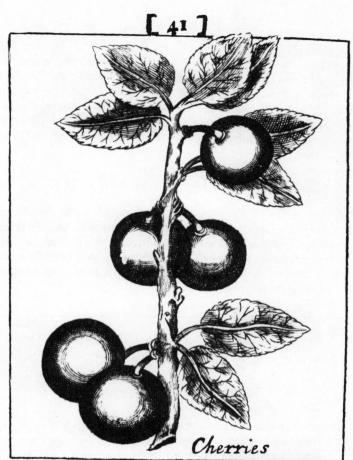

Cherries

Clarret wine, and so season it with *sugar, cinamon,* and *ginger.*

To make a close Tart of Cherries.

Take out the stones, and lay them as whole as you can in a Charger, and put *Mustard, Cinamon,* and *Sugar,* into them, and lay them into a Tart whole, and close them, then let them stand three quarters of an hour in the Oven, and then make a Syrupe of *Muskadine,* and *Damask water,* and *sugar,* and so serve it.

To make fine Pippin Tarts.

Quarter, pare, core, and stew your *Pippins* in a Pipkin, upon very hot embers, close covered, a whole day, for they must stew

softly,

softly, then put to them some whole *Cinamon*, six *Cloves*, and *sugar* enough to make them sweet, and some *Rose-water*, and when they are stewed enough, take them off the fire, and take all the Spice from them, and break them small like *Marmalade*, and having your Coffins ready made, not above an inch deep, fill them with it, and lay on a very thin cover of puffe paste, close and fit, so bake them, serve them in cold, but you must take heed you doe not over-bake them.

To make a Tart of Butter and Eggs.

Take the yolks of sixteene *Eggs* well parted from the whites, three quarters of a pound of *Butter* well Clarified, and straine it twice or thrice in a faire strainer, seasoned with *sugar* and a little *Rose water*, wherein *Spinage* first a little boyled, hath been strained, to make it green ; be sure your paste be well made, and whole, and so bake it up, and serve it.

Of Goose-Berries.

To keep Goose-Berries.

Take a handfull or two of the worser of your *Goose-Berries*, cut off their stalks and heads, and boyle them all to pieces, in a pot-tell of water, putting into the boyling thereof, halfe a quarter of *sugar*, then take the liquor, straine it through a haire strainer, and while it cooleth cut off the stalks and heads of the fairest *Goose-Berries*, being very carefull you cut not the skin of them above or below ; put them into a gally pot, and pour the liquor in after them.

Purslaine must be used as you doe the *Goose-Berries*.

The best way to Preserve Goose-Berries.

Gather them with their stalks on, cut off their heads, and stone them, then put them in scalding water, and let them stand there-in covered a quarter of an hour, then take their weight in *sugar*, finely beaten, and laying first a lay of *sugar*, then one of your *Goose-Berries*, in your Preserving Skillet or pan, till all be in, putting in
for

for every pound of *Goose-Berries*, six spoonfulls of water, set them on the embers till the *sugar* be melted, then boyle them up as fast as you can, till the Syrupe be thick enough, and cold, and then put them up. This way serves also for *Respasses* and *Mulberries*.

Of Plums.

The best way to dry Plums.

Take your *Plums* when they are full growne, with the stalks on them, but yet green, split them on the one side, and put them in hot water, but not too hot, and so let them stand three or four hours, then to a spoonfull of them, take three quarters of a pound of *sugar*, beaten very fine, and eight spoonfulls of water to every pound, and set them on hot embers till the *sugar* be melted, and after that boyle them till they be very tender, letting them stand in that Syrupe three dayes to plump them, then take them out, wash the Syrupe from them with warm water, and wipe them with a fine linnen cloath, very dry, and lay them on plates, and set them to dry in a Stove, for if you dry them in an Oven, they will be tough.

To Preserve Damsons.

Take *Damsons* before they be full ripe, but new gathered off the Tree, allow to every pound of them a pound of *sugar*, put a little *Rose-water* to them, and set them in the bottome of your pan, one by one, boyle them with a soft fire, and as they seeth strew your *sugar* upon them, and let them boyle till the Syrupe be thick enough, then while the Syrupe is yet warme, take the *Plums* out, and put them in a gally pot, Syrupe and all.

To Preserve Bullasses as green as grasse.

Take your *Bullasses*, as new gathered as you can, wipe them with a cloath, and prick them with a knife, and quaddle them in two waters, close covered, then take a pound of Clarified *sugar*, and a pint of *Apple water*, boyle them well together (keeping them well scummed) unto a Syrupe, and when your *Bullases* are

well

well dript from the water, put them into the Syrupe, and warm them three or four times at the least, at the last warming take them up, and set them a dropping from the Syrupe, and boyle the Syrupe a little by it selfe, till it come to a jelly, and then between hot and cold put them up to keep for all the year.

To Preserve Pares, Pare-Plums, Plums.

First take two pound and a halfe of fine *sugar*, and beat it small, and put it into a pretty brasse pot, with twenty spoonfulls of *Rose-water*, and when it boyleth skim it clean, then take it off the fire, and let it stand while it be almost cold, then take two pound of *Pare-plums*, and wipe them upon a faire cloath, and put them into your Syrupe when it is almost cold, and so set them upon the fire againe, and let them boyle as softly as you can, for when they are boyled enough, the kernels will be yellow, then take them up, but let your Syrupe boyle till it be thick; then put your Plums upon the fire againe, and let them boyle a walme or two, so take them from the fire, and let them stand in the vessell all night, and in the morning put them into your pot or glasse, and cover them close.

Of Medlers.

To Preserve Medlers.

Take the fairest *Medlers* you can get, but let them not be too ripe, then set on faire water on the fire, and when it boyleth put in your *Medlers*, and let them boyle till they be somewhat soft, then while they are hot pill them, cut off their crowns, and take out their stones, then take to every pound of *Medlers*, three quarters of a pound of *sugar*, and a quarter of a pint of *Rose water*, seeth your Syrupe, scumming it clean, then put in your *Medlers* one by one, the stalks downward, when your Syrupe is somewhat coole then set them on the fire againe, let them boyle softly till the Syrupe be enough, then put in a few *Cloves* and a little *Cinamon*, and so putting them up in pots reserve them for your use.

To

Medlers

To make a Tart of Medlers.

Take *Medlers* that be rotten, and ſtamp them, and ſet them upon a chaſin diſh with coales, and beat in two yolks of Eggs, boyling till it be ſomewhat thick, then ſeaſon it with *Sugar, Cinamon,*
and *Ginger,* and lay it in paſte.

Of Cucumbers.

How to keep Cucumbers.

Take a kettle big enough for your uſe, halfe full of water, make
it

it brackish with falt, boyle therein ten or twenty *Cucumbers*,, cut
in halves, then take the raw *Cucumbers*, being somewhat little,
and put them into the veffell wherein you will keep them, and
when your liquor is cold ftraine fo much of it into them, as may
keep the *Cucumbers* alwayes covered.

To keep boyled Cucumbers.

Take a kettle of water, put falt to it, boyle it well, then take
your raw *Cucumbers*, put them into it, and keep them with turning up and downe very foftly, till they be as it were per-boyled,
then take them out, and lay them afide till they be cold, then put
them up in the veffel you will keep them in, and when the liquor
is cold, ftraine it into them, till they be all covered.

To Pickle Cucumbers to keep all the yeare.

Pare a good quantity of the rindes of *Cucumbers*, and boyle
them in a quart of running water, and a pint of wine *Vineger*,
with a handfull of *falt*, till they be foft, then letting them ftand
till the liquor be quite cold, pour out the liquor from the rinds,
into fome little barrell, earthen pot, or other veffel, that may be
clofe ftopped, and put as many of the youngeft *Cucumbers* you can
gather, therein, as the liquor will cover, and fo keep them clofe
covered, that no winde come to them, to ufe all the year till they
have new ; if your *Cucumbers* be great, 'tis beft to boyle them in
the liquor till they be foft.

OF
COOKERY.

To make Snow.

Take a quart of thick *Creame*, and five or fix whites of *Eggs*,
a faufer full of *fugar* finely beaten, and as much *Rofe water*, beat
them all together, and always as it rifeth take it out with a fpoon,
then

then take a loaf of *Bread*, cut away the cruſt, ſet it in a platter, and a great *Roſemary* buſh in the middeſt of it, then lay your Snow with a Spoon upon the *Roſemary*, and ſo ſerve it.

To make Spiced Bread.

Take two pound of Manchet paſte, ſweet *Butter* halfe a pound, *Currants* halfe a pound, *ſugar* a quarter, and a little *Mace*, if you will put in any, and make it in a loaſe, and bake it in an Oven, no hotter then for Manchet.

To make Craknels.

Take five or ſix pints of the fineſt *Wheat* flower you can get, to which you muſt put in a ſpoonfull (and not above) of good *Yeſt*, then mingle it well with *Butter, cream, Roſe-water*, and *ſugar*, finely beaten, and working it well into paſte, make it after what forme you will, and bake it.

To make Veale-tooh's, or Olives.

Take the *Kidney* of a line of *Veale* roaſted, with a good deale of the fat, and a little of the fleſh, mingle it very ſmall, and put to it two *Eggs*, one *Nutmeg* finely grated, a good quantity of *ſugar*, a few *Currants*, a little *ſalt*, ſtir them well together, and make them into the form of little *Paſties*, and fry them in a pan with ſweet *Butter*.

To make a Barley Creame to procure ſleepe, or Al-mond Milke.

Take a good handfull of French *Barley*, waſh it cleane in warme water, and boyle it in a quart of fayre water to the halfe, then put out the water from the *Barley*, and put the *Barley* into a pottell of new clean water, with a *Parſley*, and a *Fennell* root, clean waſhed, and picked with *Bourage, Buglos, Violet* leaves, and *Lettice*, of each one handfull, boyle them with the *Barley*, till more then halfe be conſumed ; then ſtrayne out the liquor, and take of blanched *Almonds* a handfull, of the ſeeds of *Melons, Cucumbers, Citralls,* and *Gourds*, huſked, of each halfe a quarter of an ounce, beat theſe ſeeds, and the *Almonds* together, in a ſtone morter, with ſo much

G   *Sugar,*

Sugar, and *Rose*-water as is fit, and ſtrayne them through a cleane cloath into the liquor, and drink thereof at night going to bed, and in the night, if this doth not ſufficiently provoke ſleep, then make ſome more of the ſame liquor, and boyle in the ſame the heads, or a little of white *Poppey*.

To pickle Oyſters.

Take a peck of the greateſt *Oyſters*, open them, and put the liquor that comes from them ſaved by it ſelfe, to as much *White-wine*, and boyle it with a pound of *Pepper* bruiſed, two or three ſpoonfulls of large *Mace*, and a handfull of ſalt, till the liquor begin to waſte away, then put in your *Oyſters*, and plump them, and take them off the fire till they be cold, and ſo put them up in little barrels very cloſe.

To make very fine Sauſages.

Take four pound and a halfe of *Porck*, chop it ſmall, and put to it three pound of *Beefe* ſewet, and chop them ſmall together, then put to them a handfull of *Sage*, finely ſhred, one ounce of *Pepper*, one ounce of *Mace*, two ounces of *Cloves*, a good deale of ſalt, eight Eggs very well beaten before you put them in, then work them well with your hand, till they be throughly mingled, and then fill them up. Some like not the Eggs in them, it is not amiſſe therefore to leave them out.

To caſt all kind of Sugar works into Moulds.

Take one pound of *Barabry Sugar*, Clarifie it with the white of an Egg, boyle it till it will roule between your finger and your thumb, then caſt it into your ſtanding Moulds, being watered two hours before in cold water, take it out and gild them to garniſh a *Marchpine* with them at your pleaſure.

To make all kinde of turned works in fruitage, hollow.

Take the ſtrongeſt bodyed *Sugar* you can get, boyle it to the height of *Manus Chriſti*, take your ſtone, or rather pewter moulds, being made in three pieces, tye the two great pieces together with *Inkle*, then poure in your *Sugar* being highly boyled, turne it it round about your head apace, and so your fruitage will be hollow, whether it be *Orange*, or *Lemmon*, or whatsoever your Mould 1 oth cast, after they be cast you must colour them after their natudall colours.

To make a Sallet of all kinde of Hearbs.

Take your Hearbs and pick them very fine in faire water, and pick your Flowers by themselves, and wash them clean, then swing them in a strayner, and when you put them into a dish mingle them with *Cucumbers* or *Lemmons* pared and sliced, also scrape *sugar*, and put in *Vineger* and *Oyle*, then spread the Flowers on the top of the *sallet*, and with every sort of the aforesaid things garnish the dish about, then take Eggs boyled hard, and lay about the dish and upon the Sallet.

To make Fritter-stuffe.

Take fine flower, and three or four Eggs, and put into the flower, and a piece of Butter, and let them boyle all together in a dish or chaffer, and put in *sugar*, *cinamon*, *ginger*, and *rose* water, and in the boyling put in a little grated Bread, to make it big, then put it into a dish, and beat it well together, and so put it into your mould, and fry it with clarified Butter, but your Butter may not be too hot, nor too cold.

FINIS.

GLOSSARY

Glossary

ADDER'S TONGUE : a type of fern, *Ophioglossum vulgatum*.

AMBERGREECE: Ambergris, a grey strongly-scented substance secreted in the intestines of the sperm whale, whence it is cast up and is found floating in the sea.

AQUA VITAE: spirits of wine distilled twice or more times.

ARCHANGEL: Dead nettle, i.e. any species of *Lamium*.

BANQUETTING STUFFE: sugar-preserved fruits, sweet biscuits, jellies, marzipan and other similar confections offered at the 'banquet' or dessert course following a fine dinner.

BARBERY SUGAR: Barbary sugar, from the land of the Berbers, i.e. North Africa.

BARROWES GREASE: lard from a hog.

BENJAMIN: Benzoin, the aromatic and resinous juice of *Styrax benzoin*, a tree of Java and Sumatra.

BILE: a boil.

BITTERSWEET: Woody nightshade, *Solanum dulcamara*.

BORUS: borax, hydrated sodium tetraborate.

BRIMSTONE: sulphur.

CALAMUS: Sweet flag, *Acorus calamus*, an aromatic pond plant.

CANDY: To candy sugar means: to boil it to candy height, one of the recognised stages in sugar-boiling.

CANDY OIL: oil from Crete, formerly called Candy, and an exporter of fine olive oil.

CASTOREUM: brown oily strong-smelling substance secreted in sacs in the genital area of the beaver.

CAUDLE: warm sweetened spiced drink.

CELIDONIE: Greater celandine, *Chelidonium maius*.

CHERFOYLE: Chervil, *Anthriscus cerefolium*.

CHOLLER: choler, i.e. bile.

CITRALL: Citrul, pumpkin.

COALES: to melt butter 'upon coales' means to melt it over charcoal for controlled heat. The charcoal was burned in a small brazier, sometimes set into a flat furnace-top, but more often in the form of the freestanding chafing-dish.

COFFINS: when used as a term in cookery means: pie-cases.

CONDUICT WATER: water conveyed through conduits from a spring or other source, and so kept continually running.

CYPRIS, a sedge, *Cyperus longus*.

DIET: on p 24 means a diet drink, i.e. a drink reinforced with medicinal herbs to be taken regularly as part of the diet.

DOVE'S FOOT: Cranesbill or wild geranium, *Geranium molle*.

DRAGGONS: Dracontium, a plant of the Arum family, much used in seventeenth century medicine.

EGREMONY: Agrimony, a plant of the genus *Agrimonia*.

ELECAMPANE: a composite plant, *Inula helenium,* allied to the aster. Its root was formerly much used in medicine.

EMROIDS: haemorrhoids.

FLOS UNGUENTUM: flower of ointments.

FRENCH POX: Syphilis. Like French beans, it came to Europe originally from the Americas, but it supposedly reached the French first, and was brought to England from them.

FUSIS: probably Fustic, Venetian sumach, a shrub of the genus *Rhus*.

GALINGAL: aromatic roots of certain East Indian plants of the ginger family.

GAVANUM: probably galbanum, a gum-resin from an eastern species of giant fennel.

GLISTER: clyster, a liquid injected into the rectum.

GUIACUM: tropical American tree of the bean-caper family, yielding a greenish resin used in medicine.

GUM DRAGON: Gum tragacanth, a gum obtained from shrubs of the genus *Astragalus:*

HACKDAGGER: Hedgedagger, probably the same as Culpeper's common and winter hedgeweeds and Jack by the hedge, all varieties of *Erysimum*. The daggers are the 'seed-vessels, long slender and squared: they stand in a kind of spikes along the upper part of the stalk ... The seed ... is drying and binding, of service in all kinds of fluxes and haemorrhages, either from the bowels or from any other part'.

HUMOURS: fluids.

INKLE: broad linen tape.

IREOS ROOTS: roots of Orris, i.e. Florentine iris, having a violet-like scent, which were dried and used in perfumery.

KETTLE: metal cauldron.

LENTIVE FARINE: perhaps, lenitive farine, i.e. gently laxative meal or flour.

LETHARGY: litharge, lead monoxide.

LEYDWORT: probably Leadwort, a plant of the south European genus, *Plumbago europea.*

LIMARIA: probably Linaria, toadflax, a plant closely allied to snapdragon.

MADENWORT: Madwort, also called moonwort or healdog, a herb of the genus *Alyssum,* believed to drive out madness and to cure those bitten by mad dogs.

MANCHET: the finest white wheaten bread.

MANUS CHRISTI: a sweetmeat made from sugar boiled with rosewater to candy height, and with fragments of gold leaf then mixed into it.

MARMALADE: a thick jellied conserve of quinces and sugar.

MASE: mace, the inner coat of the nutmeg.

MASTIK: a pale yellow gum-resin from the Lentisk and other trees.

MAY BUTTER: butter left for many days exposed to the sun, which oxidized and destroyed its vitamin A, but increased its vitamin D content. It was used medicinally in the seventeenth century, often with the object of relieving pain in the joints.

MITHRIDATE: an antidote for poisoning made by a secret formula, and sold by the apothecaries. It was called after Mithridates of Pontus who, according to tradition, made himself proof against poisoning by taking small doses of various poisons to build up his resistance to them.

MUSCADINE: muscatel, a rich spicy wine.

MERCURY: probably English mercury, i.e. Good King Henry, a goosefoot of the genus *Chenopodium,* grown as a pot-herb.

MUSK: strong-smelling secretion of the male musk-deer, used in perfumery.

NEPE: Catmint, *Nepeta cataria.*

OLIBANUM: a gum-resin from a species of *Boswellia* growing in Somaliland and southern Arabia.

ORPIMENT: yellow arsenic trisulphide.

ORPINE: a purple-flowered, broad-leaved stonecrop.

PALIOLUM: 'Little hood', perhaps the species of Wolfbane or Monkshood (Aconite) which Culpeper described as Wholesome Aconite, calling it the 'medicinal one kept in the shop'. It is 'said to be very serviceable against vegetable poisons'.

PELLITORY OF SPAIN: North African and south European plant, *Anacyclus pyrethrum,* akin to camomile. The name is also applied to other similar plants, such as feverfew and yarrow.

PERBREAKING: parbeaking, i.e. vomiting.

PERROSSEN: a special resin resembling frankincense. In a book of rates of 15 July 1507 (N.S.B. Gras: *The early English customs system,* 1918, p 702), it was valued at 3s.4d. [17 p.] the hundredweight, whereas ordinary resin was 20d. [8½ p.].

PESTILENCE: Bubonic plague.

PLAINER OF DISKLOSIONS: T. Dawson's *The Good Huswife's Iewell,* 1596, from which this recipe has come perhaps at one or two removes, has PLAISTER OF DIUFLOSIUS. This was the plaster called *Diaflosmos* because one of its ingredients was mullein, Verbascum Thapsus, 'that is called flosmos', according to John Arderne. He claimed that the plaster made with mullein 'heleth wele alle woundes, thof-al thai be horrible', in his

Treatise of Fistula, 1376; and it was still a popular remedy in sixteenth-and seventeenth-century medicine. The full recipe for the plaster is too long to be quoted here (see Arderne in: Early English Text Society, O.S. 139 (1910), pp 30–31), but it included the juices of many other herbs, with olive oil, virgin wax and turpentine. The *Diaflosmos* plaster was put into the first London *Pharmacopeia* of 1618.

PLANTINE: Plantain, a plant of the genus *Plantago.*

POSNET: small cooking-cauldron, usually three-legged.

PROBATUM: 'This has been proved'.

RANKLINGS: festering.

REINS: the loins (seventeenth century); nowadays the term means: kidneys.

RHEUM: fluid.

ROCHE ALUM: rock-alum, prepared from 'alunite', i.e. basic potassium aluminium sulphate, which occurs in aluminous rocks.

ROSSEN: rosin, a by-product of the distillation of turpentine and similar tree resins.

SANICLE: woodland umbelliferous plant, *Sanicula europea.*

SAVINE: a species of juniper, *Juniperus sabina;* its tops yield an irritant volatile oil.

SERECLOATH: cerecloth, a cloth dipped in melted wax, sometimes for use as a winding-sheet, but here evidently prepared for the treatment of aching limbs.

SEA BOISE: an unidentified plant, perhaps a misprint for 'scabious'.

SEPE PROBATUM: 'This has often been proved'.

SHARE: pubis bone, at the front of the pelvis.

SHEPHARDS PURSE: Shepherd's purse, *Capsella bursa pastoris.*

SIPITS: sippets, i.e. small pieces of bread or toast.

SOARE: perhaps Share (see above).

SPERMACETI: the waxy substance which is found mixed with the oil from the head of the sperm-whale.

SPIKE: Spikenard, an aromatic balsam.

SPURGE: a plant of the genus *Euphorbia.*

STORAX: the aromatic resin of the tree *Styrax officinalis.*

STRANGUARY: painful retention, or very slow discharge, of urine.

SYRUPE GRESTA: syrup concocted from sugar and *agresto. Agresto* was the Italian form of verjuice made from sour unripe grapes (from Latin *agrestis:* raw, crude). C. Durante, *Herbario novo,* 1585, said it was obtained especially 'from the fruit of the vine called *Agresto,* on which the ripe fruit and flowers are sometimes seen simultaneously'. (See E. David, 'Agresto', *PPC* 7 (1981), pp 30–31.)

TREACLE: originally medicated honey, confected with many herbs and spices according to a prescription said to stem from the physician of the Roman emperor Nero, and taken as an antidote for poisoning. By the seventeenth century, the honey base had been replaced by molasses.

TREACLE OF GENOA: treacle made according to the recipe used in Genoa, and exported from there.

TRYED: separated out.

UNGUENTUM ROSATUM: rose ointment.

UNGUENTUM SANATIVUM: healing ointment, made according to a special recipe which appears in e.g. *A Choice Manual of Rare and Select Secrets in Physick and Chyrurgy*, 1653, formerly attributed to Elizabeth Grey, Countess of Kent (but see E. David, 'A true gentlewoman's delight', *PPC* 1 (1979), pp 43–53).

VEALE-TOCH'S: a mis-spelling of 'Veal tourtes', i.e. tarts.

VENICE TURPENTINE: turpentine from larch-tree resin, formerly shipped from Venice.

VITRIOL: hydrous sulphate of copper (blue vitriol) or of iron (green vitriol). Oil of vitriol was concentrated sulphuric acid, prepared from sulphate of iron (green vitriol).

WHITE COPPERAS: probably either anhydrous ferrous sulphate or zinc sulphate.